HOW TO MAKE MORAL AND ETHICAL DECISIONS
A GUIDE

Norman W. Wilson PhD

HOW TO MAKE MORAL AND ETHICAL DECISIONS A GUIDE

Cover Design by

www.srwalkerdesigns.com

A ZADKIEL PUBLISHING PAPERBACK

© Copyright 2021
Norman W. Wilson PhD

The right of Norman W. Wilson to be identified as author and channel of this work has been asserted by him in accordance with the Copyright, Designs and Patents Act 1988.

All Rights Reserved

No reproduction, copy or transmission of the publication may be made without written permission.

No paragraph of this publication may be reproduced, copied or transmitted save with the written permission of the publisher, or in accordance with the provisions of the Copyright Act 1956 (as amended).

Any person who does any unauthorised act in relation to this publication may be liable to criminal prosecution and civil claims for damages.

ISBN: 978 1 78695 560 9

Zadkiel Publishing
An Imprint of Fiction4All
www.fiction4all.com

This Edition
Published 2021

Also by Norman W. Wilson

TEXTBOOKS:
Butterflies and All That Jazz with Drs. James G. Massey and Arthur J Powell
Windows & Images: An Introduction to the Humanities with Drs. James G. Massey and Arthur J Powell
The Humanities: Contemporary Images

NONFICTION:
Shamanism What It's All About
DUH! The American Educational Disaster
So You THINK You Want to Be A Buddhist?
Promethean Necessity & Its Implications for Humanity
The Sayings of Esaugetuh, the Master of Breath
Activating Your Archetypes
Shamanic Manifesting
The Shaman's Journey through Poetry with Gavriel Navarro

NOVELS:
The Shaman's Quest
The Shaman's Transformation
The Shaman's Revelations
The Shaman's War
The Shaman's Genesis
The Making of a Shaman

A fundamental question regarding moral decisions is whether one accepts morality as a social mandate, a religious mandate or as something as an inherent part of humankind.
                       Author unknown

PREFACE

How to Make Moral and Ethical Decisions will not make you a more ethical person. You are either ethical or you are not. It is the intent of this text, however, to provide you opportunities to practice making ethical decisions based on standard ethical traditions. While it is necessary to recognize that no single theory provides all the answers to your moral questions, it is equally important that you recognize that each has important truths to contribute to your moral decision-making processes. It is to that end that I direct the focus of this book. Not provided is a history of ethical systems.

Explored are several of the major Western and Eastern ethical systems, which raise questions about moral behavior. You are to arrive at your own answers based on those theories. The text material provides multiple case studies as a backdrop for your practice in making moral decisions. Contemporary issues such as rape, abortion, child sexual molestation, assisted suicide, environmental concerns, medical issues, and sexual preference all come into play as a moral dilemma.

Raised for your consideration are many provocative questions: Is it ever right to lie? Does a woman have the right to her dead husband's sperm? Does that donated sperm make that child legitimate or illegitimate? Should you stop the suffering of another by helping her or him to die? If you do, are you a murderer? Should you keep your word, always? Is there such a thing as universal morality?

Where do morals come from? Finally, the ultimate question; after all, why be moral?

The traditional theories of Consequentialism and non-Consequentialism, as well as the contemporary theories of objectivism, humanitarian ethics, and idealist ethics, are basic to your understanding of moral dilemma. Because moral decision-making does not take place in isolation the presentations of theories are in a setting of application, consequently, the "Interactives" require individual participation. Ethics is a participatory experience.

I am most grateful to my many students who have so graciously allowed me to experiment on them in the design of the material for this text. Their insights have been most helpful and inspiring.

Norman W. Wilson, Ph.D.
2021

CHAPTER ONE
GETTING STARTED

Do you feel you always get into trouble because you make the wrong decision? Could it be that you simply do not know the processes involved in making good moral and ethical decisions? Decisions of any kind require an understanding of certain fundamental or basic information. Do you go out and buy a car without first knowing something about it? Do you marry someone without first knowing something about that individual? Do you play a sport without learning the rules of the game? Of course, you don't! Then why do you think you can make ethical and moral decisions without knowing something about ethics and morality? Oh, sure, you know the Commandment "Thou shall not steal" but taking home an extra note pad from the office where you work isn't stealing, is it? Nor is taking a sample or two from the open bins of candy at the grocery store, right? And it's certainly okay to taste a couple of the grapes even if you are not buying them? Wrong! It is not acceptable ethically or morally to take that which is not yours no matter its material value.

The significance of material value came home to me several years ago while I was teaching in the public sector. In a freshman English class, we were discussing William Saroyan's short story, "The Parsley Garden" in which a little boy stole a ten-cent hammer. My students thought making him work all day to pay for it was not right because the hammer wasn't worth at least five dollars. In their minds, he had not stolen anything of real value. It had no significant intrinsic value; therefore, it was not wrong. Like the woman who samples the candy in the open bins at the grocery store or pinches a couple of grapes, these young people didn't know the process in making a moral judgment. You may feel that since the hammer, candy, or grapes weren't worth very much there isn't a problem. Besides, the store can well afford a few free samples. "Big deal!" you say. Not so fast with that rationalization for inappropriate behavior.

In this chapter, I will discuss where morals come from, why you should be moral, and present some of the views on ethical behavior held by several philosophers. Also, there will be opportunities for you to practice your moral decision-making based on what these philosophers have had to say.

Where do morals come from? Aren't they just a set of rules that tell you not to do certain things? Don't rules change and doesn't it all come down to what the situation really is, anyway? Let me begin with a mild probe into your memories. Go back to your early childhood. In those memories, is there a conversation similar to this one?

Mother: "Let Sally play with one of your toys. It's not nice to be selfish."
Child: "Why?"
Mother: "Because I said so!"

If so, it was at that point that you began to learn it was a right behavior to share with others. Second, you also began to learn there is an authority you did not question. This demonstrates just one of the many moral lessons you learned from your parent(s) and or other family members. Gradually, the religious convictions and beliefs of your family group provided further moral lessons in right behavior. In the Christian religion for example, "The Ten Commandments" offer rules of behavior. "Love your neighbor as yourself," and "Do to others as you would have them do to you: are examples of two prominent Christian commands of behavior. The society, culture, or subculture in which you live provides you with moral edicts. Issues of equal rights and the treatment of minorities derive their base in social customs and traditions.

Influences on your moral and ethical beliefs:

Parents and Family
Religion
Society
Peers

Certainly, your peers influence and help shape your moral choices and actions. Even a simple statement as "everybody's going" may have right and wrong choice implications.

An issue may become a moral issue if the choices and actions you take affect any of these:

The well being of other human beings
Your own person
The well-being of animal and plant life.

Finally, the laws under which you live form a significant base for your behavior. It is wrong to take another human being's life. Exceptions are justifiable homicide and war.[1] Even here, not everyone agrees. Some oppose the legal execution of convicted criminals. Others believe war is wrong and refuse to participate in any military activity. Are there other origins for morality? Some modern writers suggest that literature, film, and television influence, and help shape moral behavior. Can you think of a literary piece, a film, or a television program that has had a profound effect on what you believe? Do programs such a "Sesame Street" or "Beavis and Butthead" tend to present moral values? Some critics think so. What do you think? If such programs do present a moral influence should they. Is this an ethical issue itself? What about the admissions by the federal government that it helped finance certain television shows that were anti-drug or anti smoking?

What makes an issue a moral issue? Your choices and actions that affect the well-being of others may make an issue a moral one. If those actions and choices produce a negative effect on another human being then you have a moral or ethical issue. However, what if what you did creates a problem for another and you didn't mean it to be that way or that what you did, created a problem for another and you didn't know your actions would produce that negative consequence? Are you still responsible for that immoral or unethical act? Why can't you just do your own thing? Is the slogan "If it feels good, do it" morally acceptable? These are perplexing questions, to say the least. One of the early lessons you learned from your parent(s) or other family members was that if you treated others morally they, in turn, treated you morally. Let's continue the previous conversation between a mother and her daughter.

Child: "Why do I have to share my toys? They're mine."
Mother: If you don't let Sally play with some of your toys she may not let you play with any of her toys."

You were taught that sharing was good. It was good because it might result in something favorable for you. This leads me to a second reason for being moral and it's closely allied with the first. You treat others poorly, they will not be cooperative, and you may not gain what you want. You are better able to get what you want when you help others get what they want. If you are a Christian, you are familiar with their "Do to others, as you would have them do to you." The final reason for being moral and ethical is that it is ultimately self-defeating if you are not.

The fact that it **is useful** summarizes the bottom line in terms of moral behavior. Of the five branches of philosophy, ethics is the one that deals specifically with how human beings treat each other. The remaining four branches are Metaphysics (the study of existence, reality), Epistemology (the study of knowledge), Aesthetics (the study of the principles of beauty), and Politics (the study of those behaviors in the area of the cultural situation). I should mention at this point that all religious systems are ethical and philosophical but not all ethical and philosophical systems are religious. The words ethics and morals are interchangeable. Some may not agree with this particular designation and may indicate a separate distinction between business ethics, for example, and morality. I address this later.

The notion that one behaves in a certain way because it may be useful may not set well with some of you. However, the very idea of usefulness brings me to one of the profound thinkers of the eighteenth century, David Hume.

DAVID HUME (1711-1776)

Hume, a Scottish philosopher, and historian had a profound effect on moral thought. He left Edinburgh University at the age of fifteen to begin an intensive independent study. From this came his complete philosophy, *A Treatise of Human Nature*, published when he was twenty-eight years old. His other works include *Philosophical Essays Concerning the* Human *Understanding, and An Inquiry Concerning the Principles of Morals.*

Hume is a transitional figure–a bridge between the common-sense school of morality and utilitarianism. Yet, what he proposes should not be considered a "moral theory" that prescribes a set of acceptable behaviors. Instead, he presents you with a scientific description. He noted that human beings make moral judgments all of the time. His question is how do human beings learn to make moral judgments, that is, how do they determine that something is good or bad? I have already alluded to one answer to that question; however, Hume offers a somewhat different point of view in answering his own questions especially "How did morality arise?" For Hume, moral judgments are in your sentiments, specifically in sentiments of approbation, that is, feelings of approval. He states that you can feel a distinction between passions of anger and moral approval or disapproval. Moral approval occurs when you see an action as good and moral;

disapproval occurs when you view an action as bad or immoral. Hume believed that moral judgments are not the result of some abstract or rational interpretation or proof. In support of his position, Hume offers the following arguments:

All moral judgments are temporally preceded and conjoined by a sentiment of approval. Hume is simply saying that when you see something as being good, you feel good about it before you actually say it is good.

One always finds a sentiment of approval upon perceiving good actions, disapproval upon perceiving bad actions. The distinctive character of this feeling of approval or disapproval is that it is aroused only by and in human beings.

Moral judgments cannot be based on rational deliberations. Here Hume is telling you that your personal feelings are projected upon whomever or whatever you approve or disapprove.

Hume makes important distinctions between judgments of fact and judgments of value. Judgments of fact, like judgments concerning the relations of ideas, can be true or false. However, judgments of taste and morals cannot.[2] Hume's position on morality may be divided into three headings, which serve as a summary.

Reason alone cannot decide moral questions
Moral sentiment decides moral questions
Moral sentiment is actuated only by what is either pleasant or useful

Hume's theory applies to all moral judgments, but there is an important distinction between "natural virtues" and what he calls "artificial virtues." Beneficence and generosity are natural virtues whereas justice is an artificial virtue. He further suggests that if there was enough of everything to go around for everybody and if there were less greed and envy, there would be no need for justice. Since, however, the real world is not this way, society needs to develop rules that each human being should observe. Justice is such a rule and is, therefore, an artificial virtue. Look at it this way. There are natural leathers from animals (natural virtues) and manufactured leathers (artificial virtues). Both have their value and are important.

According to Hume, moral decisions sometimes produce actions and sometimes prevent actions. Finally, Hume leaves you with this bit of wisdom. He says that moral behavior is not an onerous duty–it is the best part of life. That is so because morality is its own reward. It is naturally pleasant to be moral.

How then, do you evaluate moral issues? Do you base the evaluation on sentiment? You make judgments as to whether something or someone is good or bad. You evaluate actions as bad, right, or wrong. What happens in these evaluative modes of experiencing? Examine the following scenario.

You are out for an evening walk. As you, pass an apartment building, you notice that the glass sliding doors of the ground-floor apartment are open. A man, dressed in dark clothing and a mask, is sneaking into the main room. There you see a young woman, apparently asleep, on a couch. The man pulls a knife, places it against her throat as she awakens.

Would you judge this man as bad? Most of you would agree that he is bad and should be caught and punished. If you feel this way, you have made a moral judgment based on an individual's actions. Do you ever judge a person as good or bad based on appearances? What if this scenario is actually a staged scene for a film for a crime prevention-training program? You would have felt silly if you had barged in and found it to be a movie set.

Appearances can be deceiving. Basing your moral judgments on appearances may lead to poor or wrong conclusions and ultimately poor decisions. Generally, however, most moral evaluations are based on an individual's actions. To know whether someone is good or bad you first must know what actions are morally acceptable or required or are unacceptable. It is now appropriate that you consider the kinds of actions. Examine this list of actions and decide which you feel are immoral.

1. Tom slips his little brother
two joints of marijuana.
2. Sarah copies her friend's proposal for a new ad campaign and submits it as her own.
3. John told his girlfriend he had to work late and couldn't keep his date with her when actuality had a date with another woman.

4. Jean sold the young man a six-pack of beer, knowing he was not of legal age.

5. Even though he was in the office, Alex told his secretary to say he was out of town when Mr. Jones called.

Making moral judgments about the above situations involves making judgments about actions. When moral judgments about kinds of actions are made moral, principles are involved. In the first example, it is wrong for Tom to give marijuana to his little brother. The moral principle involved may be stated as "giving illegal drugs to children is wrong."

The following may seem somewhat confusing; nevertheless, the point is a very important one in understanding the concept of moral judgment. If you say, it is wrong for Tom to give marijuana to his little bother you have made a moral judgment. To claim that it is wrong to give illegal drugs to children is a moral principle rather than a moral judgment. It is the **principle** that you use to make your moral judgments about certain types of actions. The moral issue raises the question; the moral principle answers it. Using my first example, the situation may be set up in this way.

Moral Issue: Should one give marijuana to children? (The question)

Moral Principle: One should not give illegal drugs to children. (The answer)

INTERACTIVE ONE

Directions:

Using the two statements above, write the moral issue and the moral principle for each. Check your statements with those provided at the end of the chapter.

INTERACTIVE TWO

Directions:

Read the following abbreviated scenario. Assume the role of an observer. Answer the questions that follow.

Ted and his best friend are in a small boat fishing.

A gust of wind capsizes the boat. Ted is not a very good swimmer. His friend yells out that she can't swim. Ted knows that he's not a good enough swimmer to help her. To try may mean they would both drown. He desperately dog-paddles toward the shore. A man pulls him out while another swims toward the young woman. It's too late; she has gone under.

1. How did you judge Ted? Is he selfish?
2. If he chose to try to save his best friend and both drown, is he a hero for trying?
3. Is he a coward since he saved only himself?

As you well know, people do not always make the same moral judgments or accept the same moral principles. What do you do when faced with a moral decision? What about the Christian commandment, "Thou shall not judge." Are you one of those persons who, when faced with a moral dilemma, gives up, and excuses yourself by saying, "Who am I to judge?" Is that a capitulation of your responsibilities if you do? Aren't you really begging the issue? Doesn't such behavior imply that only persons with a certain kind of authority have the right to judge or make moral evaluations? Perhaps your pastor, rabbi, or priest? A teacher? A judge? God?

You make the judgments! Your questions should not be "Who am I to judge?" but rather, "Which judgment or moral principle is more reasonable?" And not everyone agrees with this position. Some people find it makes no sense to say that some moral judgments are more reasonable than others are. One person who believes that moral judgments may indeed have to be prioritized is G. E. Moore.

GEORGE EDWARD MOORE (1873-1958)

Born into a relatively well-to-do English family, George Edward Moore would eventually have a significant impact on philosophy. At age eight, he entered Dulwich College where he studied the classics. From there he went to Trinity College to study his new area of interest, philosophy. Moore became a professor at Cambridge where he remained until his retirement in 1939. An announced agnostic, Moore believed that which made right actions right was their production of more good than alternative actions. He claimed that how "good" was to be defined was the most important and basic question in all ethics.

For Moore, the most important sense of *definition* is what the parts are, and which compose a whole. In this sense, "good" has no definition. The question you must ask is what are the parts of good? There is none! Moore argued that **good** was a simple non-natural indefinable property and any attempt to connect it with a natural property involved a fallacy. In fact, he called the attempts to render parts to good as the ***naturalistic fallacy***. Many philosophers of the day were influenced by this concept, even to the point of abandoning their former beliefs. Accordingly, you are to choose those actions as priority actions that produce more good. Suppose a doctor has been working a new serum that would save thousands of new babies' lives. To perfect his serum, the doctor gives it to a hundred babies, and they all die. However, in the course of this trial run, the doctor discovered what was needed to make his serum work. Because of his efforts, thousands of new babies would now be saved. Do you think this doctor was morally right or was he morally wrong because some of his actions caused the death of one hundred human babies? Do you agree with G. E. Moore's idea that if more good is produced than by other actions, then the doctor's actions were moral, and as in this case more good was produced because more human babies were saved? If you don't agree with G. E. Moore, you are not alone. One such person who disagreed with Moore was W. D. Ross.

W.D. ROSS (1877-1971)

Ross called these duties prima facie duties. Prima facie literally means "at first glance" or "on the surface of things." According to Ross, you must generally adhere to these duties unless circumstances or reasons dictate otherwise. As applied to ethical theory, prima facie means first duties, that is, there are certain duties that you should perform before performing others. The words generally and unless have significance. They immediately notify you that Ross does not believe morals are absolute. Absolute, as it is used here, means there are no exceptions.

W. D. Ross lists certain prima facie duties that he feels everyone should adhere to in a general sense. And these, he believes, take priority over other considerations. Among the duties on his list are fidelity, justice, and reparation.3 These duties are right because they relieve human beings from suffering. Here is an interesting aside for your consideration. What if there was no suffering? Would there be any need for these moral duties? Is the implication here that for one to be moral there must be suffering that he or she can relieve?

The interest in Ross, at this point, is, however, his answer to the question, "What makes an action right?" Remember that G. E. Moore advanced the notion that an action is good if it produces more good than could have been produced by any other action. Ross, on the other hand, believes that what makes an action right is that an individual has promised to do it. Sounds simple enough doesn't it? However, what if a person has promised to kill you? Does the fact that he has promised to do so make such an act morally right? Ross's answer may be stated something like this:

Besides the duty of fulfilling promises, you have made you have a duty of beneficence that is, a duty of helping others to improve their conditions. It is not the production of more good, but that one duty is more of a duty than the other duty.

One cannot help another improve his condition by killing him consequently the promise to kill you is invalid and immoral. There is no beneficence.

You have now been briefly introduced to three philosophers that deal with ethical/moral behavior: David Hume, G. E. Moore, and W. D. Ross. Each has specific views about morality. All ethical/moral decisions must be based on an understanding of the fundamental principles involved. An understanding of what the great thinkers have said about ethics will help provide that necessary basis. Consider the following case study in light of the three ethical theories presented.

CASE STUDY 1.0 - (JEFF AND FRIENDS)

Background Data

Three young men, Jeff, Bill, and Bob have gone out for the evening to their favorite "watering hole." Jeff has agreed, ahead of time, to be the trio's designated driver and has promised to drive his two friends home when they were ready to leave.

The Scenario

At the bar, Jeff meets Glory, his newest interest. He has been trying to connect with her for over two weeks. He buys her a drink and orders mineral water for himself, remembering his promise to his buddies that he would be their designated driver. Glory wants Jeff to stay for the last dance of the evening. He agrees.

As the evening wears on, Bob and Bill decide they have had it and want to leave. Bob signals Jeff it's time for them to leave. Jeff turns to Glory.

"My friends are ready to leave. I'm their designated driver."

"But you promised to stay for the last dance. I guess I know where I stand." Glory protested.

"Hey Jeff, you coming?"

Turning, Jeff looked at his two friends; both were higher than a kite.

"Damn! Oh, what the hell?" he said to himself as he reached for Glory's hand.

INTERACTIVE THREE

Which promise did Jeff keep? Did he drive his buddies home or did he stay to have the last dance with Glory? Which do you think he should do?

Each of the three philosophers presented provides an answer. List three choices that Jeff could have made. Then, opposite each choice write the name of the philosopher whose theory of ethics would apply to that choice. The philosophers are David Hume, G. E. Moore, and W. D. Ross. You may use a philosopher more than once.

For my suggested answer to this Interactive go to the end of this chapter. Before going any further, two other aspects of morality are important for your understanding. First is the notion of **universality**. Philosophers maintain that for a principle to be considered a moral principle it must be universal. This means that it must apply to human beings in general. That is, it must be broad enough so as not to exclude anyone. It also must be consistent. The second notion deals with the **justification** of the moral judgments you make. Ah! Just what you've been waiting for. Not so fast. Justification does not mean rationalizing your behavior. Moral judgments must be sound; they must have good reasons for supporting them. If your moral judgments are based on intuition, whim, or caprice others are justified in rejecting them. How then, do you justify your moral judgments? You do so by presenting a **moral argument.** Moral arguments have three parts: two premises and a conclusion. A **premise** is a reason used to support your conclusion. A ***conclusion*** is a statement that is to be proved. Here is an example:

Tom drives while intoxicated.
It is wrong to endanger others.
Therefore, it is wrong to drive while intoxicated.

In making moral judgments, three areas must be considered.
What are the facts?
What is the moral principle?
What do the words mean?

> Tom's intoxication endangers others.
> Beliefs about the facts
> Tom has a drinking problem.
> The Moral Principle

This shows how a moral argument would be set up. Moral argumentation should always be based on sound reasoning. If it is not, others are justified in ignoring or dismissing it. But what if a moral judgment is based on feelings–sentiments? Examine the following case study and then answer the questions under the Interactive.

CASE STUDY 1.1 (JIM AND AMANDA)

Background Data:

Jim and Julia had promised their daughter, Amanda, a trip to Walt Disney World. Jim, a virologist, has been working on a new vaccine to fight a particular type of cancer.

The Scenario:

The director of the laboratory where Jim works is anxious for Jim to complete his tests. Successful tests mean millions of dollars for the company and perhaps a Nobel for Jim. The boss pushes Jim to work late and to come in on Saturday, the very day that he and Julia were to take Amanda to Walt Disney World.

Jim goes to work. Amanda is heartbroken and spends most of her day in her room.

INTERACTIVE FOUR

Answer each of the following questions. Answers to questions 1 and 3 are at the end of the chapter.

1. Assume G. E. Moore's theory about morality. Defend Jim's broken promise to his daughter.

2. In your **opinion,** is there a greater good involved in this scenario? If so, what is that good? Briefly, explain why it is the greater good.

3. Apply W. D. Ross's prima facie duties to this scenario. How does it differ from Moore's approach? Which approach do you prefer? Why?

When you say something is good as a judgment, what does the word "good" mean? One philosopher who attempted to deal with that type of judgment is Thomas Hobbes.

THOMAS HOBBES (1588-1679)

Hobbes holds that judgments such as "this is good" can be analyzed into "I desire this." From his point of view, moral language merely uses another form of words to speak about one's desires, inclinations, and feelings. On the surface, this may seem strange coming from a man who viewed people as selfish and violent. His feelings were so strong that he often quoted the Roman poet, Plautus (c.254-184 BCE), who said, "Homo lupus homini" meaning "Man is the wolf of man."

For Hobbes, morality is grounded in self-interest. People according to Hobbes act solely to achieve gratification and to avoid harm. This attitude is not too dissimilar to the Hedonist of ancient Greece. The earlier make-believe conversation between a mother and her daughter illustrates the Hobbesian principle. He tells you that the only effective reason for being moral is that it serves your interests. He argues that justice and gratitude, for example, function in your life as a defense against strife and disorder. According to

Hobbes, you conform to these elements because of the dictates of nature. Moral requirements, after all, require the backing of force. He puts it this way, "Covenants (agreements) with the sword are better than words." In essence, he put little faith in human nature.

Hobbes certainly was not the first philosopher to have had these feelings about human beings. You may very well feel that a person's word is of little value and that human beings, in general, are not too worthy. An earlier thinker than Hobbes, Mencius, the great Confucian philosopher felt much the same way.

MENCIUS (371-289 BCE)

Mencius, actually Meng-tzu, was born in what is now called Shantung Province in China. Reports claim that he was taught by the grandson of Confucius. Despite his negative assessment of the situation of his day, Mencius believed, as did Confucius before him, that mankind from its very beginnings was basically good. He felt mankind had become corrupted by life and circumstance. For Mencius, the upright or good life can be found only within the human being himself. And the path to this upright life must include suffering and difficulty. This notion of difficulty and suffering is to be considered the way to develop independence, excellence, mental alertness, courage, and quietude of spirit– all of which are considered virtues. The idea that difficulty and suffering develop virtues is also found in early Greek philosophy as well as in modern philosophy. The twentieth-century philosophy of Existentialism accepts the notion that the world is hostile and filled with anxiety and pain, out of which, develop virtues or values.

In other words, you have to pay attention to your own individual natural goodness and it will develop and rule your life. ***The development of your character is the most important moral task that you have.*** From its development comes benevolence which Mencius considered to be the primary virtue. And finally, Mencius believed that you have certain duties that have to be met, but to fulfill these duties you, first of all, must be virtuous.

You may feel this sounds similar to W. D. Ross's prima facie duties and you are correct. Not only are the concepts similar but so is their subjectivity. Theories that are classified as ***subjectivistic*** are frequently viewed as being void of rational reasoning. By this, critics of the theories mean that there is o scientific basis for making decisions or judgments in the area of morals or ethics. Modern culture is scientifically based.

Theodore Roszak[4] points out that one of the chief identifying characteristics of modern American culture is its objectivity. Roszak brings into focus the notion of an objective consciousness, one that has been cleansed of all subjectivity. Do you think it is possible to be totally non-subjective in your relationships?

On the other hand, in ethics, those theories which advance the notion of being free of all subjectivity are called *objectivistic*. These theories hold that a statement is true or false in exactly the same way as when you say that one plus one equals two. It is either true or it isn't. Classical ethics provides excellent examples. Plato, one of the great philosophers of all times, tells you that such statements as 'this is good" are not about any one's feelings or desires because there exists in the world a certain quality called "goodness." John Stuart Mill is an example from a more modern period.

JOHN STUART MILL (1806-1873)

John Stuart Mill, a remarkable person, had by the age of three, mastered Greek, by eight, Latin, and by twelve, he had read some of the great literary and philosophical works of his day. His principal works include *A System of Logic* (1843), *Utilitarianism* (1846), and *The Subjection of Women* (1869). Mills is a proponent of the objectivistic ethical theory called *Utilitarianism*. We will discuss Mill again in another chapter but for now, it is enough to say that Utilitarianism is not his original brainchild, but rather that of Jeremy Bentham (1748-1832). Briefly, Utilitarianism is an effort to create a principle for determining when any given action is right or wrong. This is the Principle of Unity: An action is right so far as it tends to produce the greatest happiness for the greatest number.[5]

The essence of Utilitarianism is that it stresses the effects that an action has or causes. If an action produces more beneficial effects than it does harmful ones, then it is right otherwise, it is wrong. Utilitarianism meets the requirements for an objectivistic classification because it does not claim that moral judgments are true or false. Later you will see that that Utilitarianism has the characteristics of Consequentialism, a sub-classification. There are seven sub-classifications of ethical theories: Naturalistic, Non-Naturalistic, Emotivist, Deontological, Consequentialism, Non-Consequentialism, and Motivist. Each of these will be explored ever so briefly simply as a point of information for you.

Thomas Hobbes, introduced earlier, presents a good example of an ethical theory that may be classified as Naturalistic. Naturalistic theories claim that moral judgments, true or false, may be reduced to some natural science, namely psychology, and are disguised ways of making psychological statements. On the other hand, a theory that claims that moral judgments are true or false and are not reducible to any natural science is called Non-Naturalistic. Christian ethics is an example of Non-Naturalistic classification. It holds that moral judgments are expressions of the Divine Will and this is frequently expressed as "Do what God commands" or "God is the source." Please note that long before the advent of Christianity, Greek philosopher Plato asked, "Whether actions are made right by the fact that God commands them, or whether God commands acts because they are independently right?" This is a plaguing question, to say the least. Religious leaders, as well as other philosophers, have pondered this question for hundreds of years. The Emotivist Theory claims that moral judgments are neither true nor false, but are merely expressions of the **feelings** of those who make them. Such expressions cannot be verified by scientific study. Incidentally, they cannot be proven false by science either. Some philosophers state that you do not have statements of morals here, but only expressions of certain kinds of emotions– not much different from a grunt or an "ah" after devouring a hot fudge sundae or quaffing down your favorite brew.[6] Such statements have no relationship to moral behavior. One philosopher who believes moral statements are meaningless is A. J. Ayer.

A. J. AYER (1910-1989)

Ayer, a long time professor at Oxford University, is the author of several books in philosophy. Among these are *Language, Truth and Logic*, and *Philosophical Essays.* His ethics may be classified as Emotivist because he believes that moral statements are not statements of fact and are not true or false. They are similar to the boos expressed at a sports event. His *verifiability principle* argues that any statement is neither true by definition nor verifiable through your five senses, is by necessity meaningless. Accordingly, such statements as "that is good" or "that is bad" cannot be defined. Furthermore, Ayer rejects Moore's notion that goodness or badness is simple and indefinable. He also rejects W. D. Ross' idea of intuiting what is right or wrong. The final word from Ayer is that moral statements are meaningless.

By now you can see that the great philosophers all had difficulties in agreeing on what were good and bad behaviors. is it any wonder that you may have experienced problems in today's hectic world? If the great minds can't come to terms with fundamental issues what chance do you have? Understanding that other before you had significant questions about moral and ethical behavior and that, they too, struggled for answers will help you in your own moral decision-making processes. As I stated earlier, making correct moral decisions is never easy but you may take some small comfort in knowing that you are not alone, that others before you have faced similar issues. One of the great minds who set the whole world of philosophy on its ear was Immanuel Kant.

IMMANUEL KANT (1724-1804)

Immanuel Kant, born at Konigsberg, Germany, taught at the University of Konigsberg. It is said that he was so committed to his own duty-bound ethical system that the town's people set their watches by his daily walks. His monumental work, *The Foundations of the Metaphysic of Morals*, written in 1785, contains his thinking on ethical behavior. Rejecting both the views of Francis Hutchenson (1649) and David Hume (1711), Kant advanced the idea that morals are not contingent but absolute, and their imperatives (duties) are not hypothetical but categorical (unconditional). These duties are unconditional, universal, and valid and do not depend on possible consequences. Kant's formulations are called *categorical imperatives* or unconditional duties.

Kant would have you act on a maxim or apothegm[7] if you could will it into universal law. If you cannot consistently will that, everyone would, do some type of action then that action would be morally wrong. This imperative is the criterion by which all other principles are judged. One of Kant's arguments is that you cannot will that everyone makes lying promises. If everyone did, the very institution of promising would collapse because the whole notion of promise rests on keeping the promise or at least on the intention of doing so. Being able to make something universal is Kant's first categorical imperative.

His second categorical imperative states that human beings should be treated as ends and never merely as means. In other words, an individual should never be exploited, manipulated, or used as a means to achieve one's own ends. Not everyone agrees with this imperative, especially Friedrich Nietzsche (1844-1900) who rejects the idea on the base of inegalitarianism.[8] We will say more about Kant under Motivist Theory.

The fifth sub-classification is the *Consequence Theory*. Consequence Theory claims that the rightness or wrongness of an act depends on the effects that the action(s) produce. A good example of this sub-classification comes from the Ancient Greek philosopher, Epicurus.

EPICURUS (342-270 BCE

The Hedonist (from the Greek word *hedone*, meaning pleasure) believed that an act was good or bad depending upon the amount of pleasure or pain that act produced. The man credited with the authorship of this philosophy is Epicurus, an Athenian. Sometimes Hedonism is called Epicureanism after its author. A life of pleasure sounds wonderful. One of the things many people tend to forget about Epicurus is his belief that if a person pursued pleasure too arduously, pain would follow. Consequently, he advised a life of moderation. He listed very few things as pleasurable. Among those were friendship and good conversation. Marriage is listed as a bad pleasure. For the Hedonist, a moral act is one that produces more pleasure than it does pain. Eating chocolate until you were sick would be a bad thing and immoral. "Eat, drink, and be merry" is not the Hedonist motto. Moderation in all things is.

The sixth sub-classification is ***Non-Consequentialism***. Non-Consequentialism holds that moral behavior is not based on consequences of any given act, but rather, it is based on some other moral standard and is generally considered a higher standard.

An example of a Non-Consequential classification would be the Divine Command

Theory. This theory very simply stated, for now, states that morality comes from a Divine source.

The last sub-classification of moral theories is called Motivist. **Motivist** theories promote the idea that the rightness or wrongness of an act depends on the motive for committing the act. Once again, Immanuel Kant's ethical theory may serve as an excellent example. Kant, remember, is more interested in motivation(s) and not just in the act and its possible consequences. Because he is, his theory of "duty ethics" may be classified as Motivist. Nothing in this world according to Kant can be called good without qualification except what he calls *Good Will.* A "good will" is good neither because of what it does or affects, nor for the attainment of some specified end, but simply by the virtue of the act that it is good in and of itself. And doesn't that open up a whole can of worms? More will be said about this later.

CASE STUDY 1.2 - (ROB & DR. ARNOLD)

Background Data:

Rob is a nineteen-year-old college student whose parents were divorced when he was ten years old. He accepts his stepfather but there is a cool distance between them. Frequently Rob's six-foot frame and charming good looks mask the turmoil he feels. His first sexual experience at fourteen with his neighbor's eighteen-year-old daughter had been less than wonderful. At college, he finds that each week he is drawn closer to Dr. Arnold, his history professor. There is an uneasiness about his feelings.

The Scenario:

As was his custom Rob arrived early for Dr. Arnold's history class. He eased himself into a seat in the front row, stretched out his long legs, and settled in for the morning's lecture. He especially liked the way the professor lectured.

Suddenly Rod realized the class was over and that he was still in his seat. He felt somewhat awkward as he began to put away his class notes. Dr. Arnold was speaking to him.

"Rob, I picked up a couple of videos on the Civil War. As I recall that's your favorite American historical period, isn't it?"

"Yes. Yes, sir." Rob stammered as he felt his face redden.

"Well," continued Dr. Arnold, "I was wondering if you'd like to stop by tonight and watch them? We could send out for a pizza and have a couple of beers if you like?"

Rob felt a flush creep along the back of his neck as he looked at the handsome man standing in front of him.

"You can stay the night if you like. Got plenty of room." Dr. Arnold continued.

INTERACTIVE FIVE

This case involves several issues. It may have emotional overtones for you or it may not. Look at its ingredients. Answer each of the following questions. Note to parents: If you do not wish this scenario, please feel free not to and to substitute one of your own. Similar situations involving students in elementary school and their teachers have made headlines.

Based on the information provided, do you feel that Rob should accept his professor's invitation?

There are two legal issues involved. What are those legal issues? Can they also be an ethical/moral issue?

Which of these two legal issues is most relevant to Rob's current situation?

Of the several ethical theories that have briefly been explored which one do you think **best** fits this case?

Explain why you chose the theory you did.

GLOSSARY OF TERMS

Aesthetics--- The study of the principles of beauty in art.

Consequence Theory--- The rightness or wrongness of an act depends on the effects that act have.

Deontological Theory--- The rightness or wrongness of an act depends on what kind of an act it is.

Emotivist Theory--- Moral judgments are neither true nor false. They are merely expressive of the feelings of the individual making them.

Epistemology--- The study of knowledge.

Ethics--- The study of moral behavior and moral judgment.

Metaphysics--- The study of existence; of reality.

Motivist Theory--- The rightness or wrongness of an act depends on upon the motive from which the act was done.

Naturalist Theory--- Moral judgments are true or false and they are reducible to concepts of some natural science, generally psychology.

Non-Naturalistic Theory--- Moral judgments are true or false, but they cannot be reduced to some natural science.

Objectivist Theory--- Statements of moral judgments are true or false in the same way as one plus one equals two. It either is or is not true.

Philosophy--- literally means "the love of wisdom."

Politics--- Involves the behavior toward others in a cultural and institutional setting.

Prima facie--- Literally means "on the surface," "first duty." Duties that have a priority over other duties.

Subjectivist Theory--- Moral judgments are neither true nor false and are always about the psychology of the person making them.

SUGGESTED READINGS

Bradley, F.H. 1972. "Why Should I Be Moral?" **Ethical Studies**. London: Oxford University Press, 53-74.

Goswami, Amit. 1995. "An Idealist Theory of Ethics." **The Self-Aware Universe**. New York: G. P. Putman's Sons. 256-268.

Hospers, John. 1982. **Human Conduct, 2nd ed.** New York: Harcourt, Brace, and World.

Moore, G. F. 1903. **Principa Ethics**. New York: Cambridge University Press.

Pojman, Louis. 1900. **Ethics: Discovering Right and Wrong**. Belmont, CA: Wadsworth.

Ross, W. D. 1930. **The Right and the Good**. London: Oxford University Press.

Taylor, Paul W. 1972. **Problems of Moral Philosophy 2nd ed**. Belmont, CA. Dickenson.

Titus, Harold H. & Morris Keeton. 1973. **Ethics Today**. New York: Van Nostrand.

White, James E. 1985. **Contemporary Moral Problems**. St. Paul: West.

SUGGESTED ANSWERS TO

INTERACTIVE ONE:

Item 1: Should one use another's work as his/her own?
One should not use another's work as his/her own.
Item 2: Should one tell a lie to do something else?
One should not lie.
Item 3: Should one provide alcoholic beverages to minors?
One should not provide alcoholic beverages to minors.
Item 4: Should one ask another to lie for him/her?
One should not ask another to lie.

INTERACTIVE TWO:

1. Personal opinion here. Some of you may view Ted as a selfish individual, caring only for his own person; others may view Ted as having done the correct thing knowing that he was not a strong swimmer. There have been actual cases in which the surviving person has been charged with murder. This has also been the subject of film, the most famous being the Montgomery Cliff/Elizabeth Taylor film, *A Place in the Sun*.

2. Personal opinion here. Some of you may view Ted as a hero because he sacrificed himself to try and save another person's life.

3. Personal opinion here. No, Ted's intent was to get help in rescuing his friend.

CASE STUDY 1.0: INTERACTIVE THREE

Possible Choices and Ethical Theories Involved
1. Jeff stayed for the last dance. G. E. Moore
2. Jeff took his friends home. W. D. Ross
3. Jeff took Glory with him as he drove his friends home. David Hume

CASE STUDY 1.1: INTERACTIVE FOUR

According to G. E. Moore, those actions that produce more good than non-good are moral actions. Because Jim's work has the potential of saving many lives, he is morally correct in breaking his promise to his daughter, Amanda.

Personal opinion here. Yes, we may say there is a "greater good" involved in this case study because of the possibility of lives being saved. It is a greater good than the pleasure of taking one's daughter to Disney World. Here the good of the greatest number outweighs the good of one. Not everyone would agree with this, as you will see in my suggested answer to question three below.

W. D. Ross's prima facie duties may be applied to this case because a parent's first duty is to his child. It differs from G. E. Moore's theory because it allows for the establishment of priorities in dealing with specific events. (The "why" aspect of this question requires your personal opinion.)

CASE STUDY 1.2: INTERACTIVE FIVE

Answers will vary on this question.

There are two legal issues presented or alluded to in this case. The first is the sexual liaison Rob had with his neighbor's eighteen-year-old daughter when he was fourteen; the second involves the offer of beer by Dr. Arnold, the history professor. There are both legal and moral issues implied. However, only the second issue is relevant to the case study. One of the problems you face when making moral/ethical decisions is sorting out the irrelevant issues. The question you must always ask is "Who has the moral dilemma?" In this scenario, is it Rob or Dr. Arnold? It is Rob!

The offer of beer by the professor to an underage student is not only illegal but also immoral.

This case may be examined from at least two points of view, as can most situations: that of Rob and that of Dr. Arnold.

I will begin with Rob. According to the information presented in the scenario. His history professor fascinates Rob yet at the same time, he is not entirely comfortable with his feelings. The clues to his feelings lie in his distance from his stepfather, in his less than satisfactory sexual encounter with his neighbor's older daughter, in his remaining after the lecture, and in his blushing when he is addressed by Dr. Arnold. The issues for Rob include the invitation to spend the night at Dr. Arnold's, the offer of beer when he knows he is underage, and whether or not he should follow his developing feelings for the professor. These create a moral dilemma for him. Because we do not know Rob's answer/decision, it is difficult to assign a specific moral theory to his situation. For the sake of an example, Hobbes' theory could be applied. He said desires, feelings are grounded in self-interest; people act solely to achieve gratification.

On the surface, Dr. Arnold provides enough information to formulate an application of an ethical theory. His offer of beer to a minor is illegal. His offer to have Rob spend the night raises certain professional issues. Is such an offer appropriate professorial behavior? The professor has certainly gone out of his way to get videos of a particular historical period in which Rob has expressed an interest; he has offered food and beer as well as the invitation to spend the night. These might suggest an interest other than one that is academic on the part of Dr. Arnold. He appears to be setting the stage for his own advantage. Immanuel Kant's theory applies here. He has stated that one should treat persons as ends unto themselves and not as means to an end. Dr. Arnold's approach to Rob is to use him as a means to his own personal satisfaction, therefore, his behavior is immoral. However, is this all there is? No! It appears on the surface that we can make this tidy little judgment about Dr. Arnold but that is not the end of the story. First, the motivation for Dr. Arnold's behavior is not established. He simply may be a dedicated teacher who goes the extra mile to help his students. Additionally, we have no evidence to suggest that Dr. Arnold knows that Rob is not of legal age.

I have included this scenario to demonstrate making moral decisions is not an easy task. Also, it should not be taken lightly. It is emotional involvement in the moral decision making processes that frequently clouds the issues and makes the decision(s) all the more difficult to make. How do you feel your responses stacked up to mine?

CHAPTER TWO
CONSEQUENTIALISM

You most likely have heard the old saying, "play with fire and you'll get burned," As long as it has been around, it still expresses the primary concern of Consequentialism. Consequentialists theories are based on a concern with the effects actions produce. Traditionally, the consequence theories are called *Teleological Theories*. Consequence theories may be divided into two major groups: *ethical egoism* and *utilitarianism*. Both of these hold that individuals ought to act in ways that would bring about good consequences. They differ as to who should benefit. The ethical egoists state that people out to act in their own self-interests; whereas, the Utilitarians believe that human beings out to act in the best interests of *all* human beings... Both may end up acting in the same way, but for different reasons. This is not dissimilar to two people driving to the same city–each going the same route, but for different reasons.

Ethical Egoism

For practical purposes, it is beneficial to divide ethical egoism into three specific forms.

Acting in your own self-interests with **everyone** else acting to support **your** interests

Acting in your own self-interests, but you make no claim as to how others should act

Everyone should always act in their own self-interests regardless of others' interests **unless** those interests serve their own interests as well.

Note that the word **everyone** is an all-inclusive term. It implies that the theory has application for all human beings. In the first form of ethical egoism, sometimes given the name of Individual Ethical Egoism, the implication is that everyone else exists for your benefit and yours alone. You claim this as part of your being. Small children often greet their parents or close relatives with gleeful cries of "What did you bring me?" Freud called this the "king-baby complex." In an adult, it is egocentricity. Admittedly, all of you have, at one time or another wished that everyone existed just for your benefit. The difference comes from the fact that most human beings do not continue to operate in this manner. There are exceptions, and I'm sure you know the type.

The second type of ethical egoism, even though it still advocates that you pursue your own self-interests, makes no claim about how other human beings should act. It does not say that others should exist for your benefit. Can you imagine the myriad of problems developing if everyone only sought their own self-interests at the neglect of others?

The third approach to ethical egoism is an attempt to universalize the theory. Remember, for something to be universal it must apply to human beings in general. In this case, everyone is to follow his or her own self-interests. A word of caution here, even though this sounds like it would result in total social chaos, do not assume that people would not cooperate in order to secure their desire goals.

One modern philosopher who supports a universal ethical egoism is the author and playwright, Ayn Rand. You may be familiar with some of her literary works: *The Fountain Head, We the Living,* or *Atlas Shrugged.*

AYN RAND (1905-1985)

Ayn (rhymes with nine) Rand was born in Leningrad, Russia (now St. Petersburg). Repulsed by the Communist takeover in Russia, Rand fled to the United States at the age of twenty. Here she became one of the most influential philosophers of the twentieth century. Her ethical egoism, which she called Rational Ethical Egoism, is presented in several of her works. For a quick reference read *The Virtue of Selfishness* [9] or *For the New Intellectual*[10].

Rand, an excellent example of an outstanding woman philosopher, believes that the first right that humankind has is the right of the ego. She claims man's first duty is to himself. His primary moral principle is never placing his main goals within others. Further, man's moral obligation is to do whatever he wishes provided those wishes do not depend primarily on others. Rand is making an eloquent argument for the independent ego. She tells you that you can sit down to a community meal, but you cannot digest it in a community stomach–it's an individual thing. Human beings think alone. For her, independence is the only measure of virtue and or value and *tha*t independence refers to the ego.

Ayn Rand uses the concept of the value or virtue of selfishness in a special way. She disregards the general usage of the word, selfish. Selfishness does not mean evil or greediness. It refers to dignity, self-wroth. It means the right of every human being to be happy in his or her own being. Isn't that one of the inalienable rights guaranteed to all of you by the United States Constitution?

Rand is all-inclusive in her use of the word **everyone**. As with other moralists, she leaves the choice up to the individual. "The Objectivist ethics holds man's life as the standard of value . . . and his own life as the ethical purpose of every individual man."[11] Remember that Thomas Hobbes discussed earlier, also believed that morality was ultimately grounded in self-interest.

Utilitarianism

Utilitarians believe you ought to act in ways that will bring about good consequences, and that you ought to act in the interests of all human beings. "The greatest good for the greatest number" is a phrase usually applied to the major beliefs of the Utilitarians. Their name has its root in the word *utility*, meaning usefulness. An act, which has utility in bringing about good ends, is moral. This includes following rules (principles) which produce the greatest good for the greatest number. *Good* is defined as happiness. Some ethicists divide Utilitarianism into two types: *Act Utilitarianism* and *Rule Utilitarianism.* For some, this seems to be a case of splitting hairs. If one follows a rule one is committing an act. For example, if you chose to follow the rule "Thou shall not kill" you are acting in that you do not kill. Jeremy Bentham (1748-1832) was the originator of Utilitarianism; however, it was John Stuart Mill that brought his concepts to full measure.

JOHN STUART MILL (1806-1873)

After suffering a breakdown, Mill realized that Bentham's Utilitarianism was too restrictive with its insistence upon the quantitative analysis of pleasure and pain. What human being could quantify every pleasure and pain they experience and still realize they had the experience, to begin with? Always cognizant of the human condition, Mill in *Utilitarianism* (1863) redefined Bentham's ethical system making it less stringent. He began with the Utility Principle[12], which states that actions that produce happiness are right, and those that do no produce happiness are wrong. This emphasis on actions and their results makes Mill's theory of ethics one of consequence and therefore, places it as a Consequentialist Theory of ethics.

A natural question at this juncture is "What does Mill mean by happiness?" Simply, happiness is intended pleasure and the absence of pain. Like the Hedonist of early Greece, Mill insists that some kinds of pleasures are more desirable and more valuable than other kinds of pleasures. Quality must also be a part of the judgment. Implied here is that levels of things exist and some levels are better than others are. Mill says, "It is better to be a human being dissatisfied than a pig satisfied; better to be a Socrates dissatisfied than a fool satisfied." He establishes the human being at a higher level of existence and even within that existence; he determines different levels of that existence. Certainly, there are other questions. How do you judge what is right or wrong? Do you base your judgments of right or wrong on intuition, deduction, trial, and error, or on your feelings? According to Mill, you do not have a direct knowledge of the moral value of any given act; there is no place for intuition in morality. However, Mill does not deny the role of feelings, convictions, et cetera. Moral judgments are a natural outgrowth and can be brought to a high level of development. Isn't that one reason for the pronouncements from religious leaders and for taking courses in ethics? Isn't that one of the reasons why you are reading this book?

Problems:

The Consequentialist theories of ethics are concerned with the outcome of actions. The outcome of an action determines its morality. As with all ethical theories, there are some practical problems, and I would be negligent if I didn't point them out. One such problem has to do with the issue of determining what would be a good consequence for others. What is the basis for determining which set of consequences would be right or wrong for all human beings? Normally, you would probably agree with this statement, "Do unto others as you would have them do unto you." But just for argument's sake re-examine this statement in terms of its implications. There are two assumptions implied in this statement. The first is the assumption that the other person(s) will want or need the same thing(s) as you do. And that may not always be true. The problem is the "Golden Rule" does not tell you what you should do—how you should act. It simply provides you a way of testing what you have decided to do against the effect that decision would have on you if you were the recipient of the decision or act(s). The second assumption is you know how to act when in reality; you may not.

A second problem area of Consequentialist theories involves the necessity to start over again in the decision-making processes for determining food or bad consequences for each set of new acts or decisions. This may create a lack of consistency in your behavior. If a theory of behavior is to work there needs to be a certain level of consistency. It cannot be as changeable as the weather. Furthermore, it would be most difficult to teach such a theory if there were not rules or guidelines to follow. On what basis would an inexperienced young person determine if his or her acts would result in good or bad consequences? Through trial and error? That could be costly. Just how are you to determine all of the consequences of any given act? Suppose you accept the moral principle, "Never kill anyone except in self-defense" as viable and as being acceptable behavior. Does this cover the execution of criminals, abortion, euthanasia, or suicide? Not everyone thinks so. In defense of Utilitarianism, one may say it is an improvement over ethical egoism in that it does attempt to take into consideration all human beings.

Before leaving the Consequentialist classification of ethical theories, there is one more theory for consideration, the theory of *Altruism*. You now this as giving a helping hand. For the Altruist, morality consists of concern for and the active promotion of the interest of others. It involves selflessness and the willingness to sacrifice yourself for others. It is similar to Utilitarianism in that it advocates the greatest good for the greatest number. It does not judge an act good or bad depending upon the utility the act has in producing goodness or badness. An Altruist relieves the suffering to relieve suffering; not because it will produce a degree of happiness. There is a duty of goodwill or as Ross calls it, a "duty of beneficence." Perhaps the biblical statement, "You are your brothers' keeper" best characterizes the altruistic point of view. The most adamant critic of Altruism is Ayn Rand who claims man is not an object of sacrifice. Think for a moment. For the Altruist to go about relieving suffering, there has to be someone suffering. Do you think it is right for people to suffer so others can come and relieve them of that suffering? Some public schools, colleges, and universities are now requiring a service component for graduation. If it is required, is it altruism? Would you be willing to serve, without pay, in some capacity in your community?

Read the following case study and then follow the directions given under the Interactive.

CASE STUDY 1.3 (ANDREW)

Background Data

Andrew, a forty-five-year-old bachelor wants a son. He has never been married and is not particularly comfortable around women. He doesn't do a lot of dating. His several attempts at adopting failed. Andrew is the CEO of his own very successful electronics company.

The Scenario

In desperation, Andrew took out an ad in a newspaper in a neighboring city. The ad read as follows:

Wanted. Woman willing to have my child.
Must be of good character and in good health.
Must be willing to have a complete medical
Examination. Will pay $10,000 upfront and
All medical costs and prenatal care. I am stable,
Clean, healthy, and non-abusive. No color
Barriers. No artificial insemination.

Twenty-five women responded to Andrew's ad and he made his choice. Nine months later, the woman gave birth to a healthy nine-pound boy. Andrew was delighted and was anxious to pick up his son. He had arranged for a full-time nurse, baby furniture, toys, clothes, and food.

Andrew went to the hospital to pick up his son. Entering the room where the woman and child were, he found her sitting in a wheelchair, suitcase beside her, and no baby in sight. A man was standing near her.

"Where's my son," Andrew demanded as he looked at the woman.

"I've changed my mind."

"What do you mean you have changed your mind? Andrew felt his anger. "Who is this," he asked pointing at the man standing behind the wheelchair.

"My attorney. He says I don't have to give up my baby. The contract I signed is not legal. I have my rights."

"Wrong. You don't have any rights. You signed a legal and binding contract."

"That's immaterial," said the man behind the wheelchair.

"You stay out of this. Look, you want more money. I've already paid you ten thousand dollars. How much more do you want?"

"I just want my baby," she replied.

Furious over these developments, Andrew yelled, "I'll see you rot in hell before I let you keep my son."

He stormed out of the hospital.

INTERACTIVE SIX

Directions:

Complete the following questions.
What is the primary moral issue?
What is the primary moral principle?
What are four alternatives?
What is the implied outcome?
What is the ethical theory involved in this scenario? Give your reason(s) for selecting the theory you did.
What is your preferred outcome? Explain why you made the choice you did.

CASE STUDY 1.4 (ELLEN)

Background Data

Ellen Adams[13] made an offer on a house. She gave her broker a check for $10,000 as earnest money. Her broker was an officer and the qualifying broker for a brokerage corporation. He had obtained the contract for the sale of the property and the title company was entrusted with Ellen's $10,000. The deal collapsed because of the seller's nonperformance.

Ellen requests her money back

Her broker had advised her to sign a release.

The Scenario

Ellen arrived at her broker's office at the appointed time. There, much to her dismay, the release had already been prepared; stating the broker and the seller would share the ten thousand dollar deposit.

"I want the release from the offer to buy changed. Put in there the deposit is to be returned to the buyer."

"Fine," the broker replied. "I'll type it in right now and remove the other clause."

Without checking the newly added statement to the release, Ellen signed it. As soon as she left the office, the broker removed the inserted line about returning the deposit to the buyer. He then faxed the release to the title company asking for the disbursement of the ten thousand dollars.

When Ellen did not receive her money back, she sent a written demand to the broker that her money should be returned. He ignored her request. She sued.

The court awarded a judgment against the broker for the ten thousand dollars and fined him court costs as well as Ellen's attorney fee.

INTERACTIVE SEVEN

Directions

Complete the remainder of the Case Study 1.4 by identifying each of the following:
Primary Moral Issue
Primary Moral Principle
Alternatives
Preferred Alternative
Ethical Theory Involved
Justification of choice of theory you selected.

***

GLOSSARY OF TERMS

Altruism. . . Concern for and the promotion of the interests of others; selflessness

Ethical Egoism. . . People ought to act in their own self-interests

Utilitarianism. . . Everyone should act in the best interest of all human beings; the greatest good for the greatest number.

Utility. . . Usefulness; practical application

Utility Principle. . . Action, which produces happiness, is right; action, which produces unhappiness, is wrong.

SUGGESTED READINGS

Mackie, J. L. *Ethics: Inventing Right and Wrong*. Middlesex. England. Penguin, 1977.

Mill, J. S. *Utilitarianism*. Baltimore. Penguin Books, 1982

Moore, G. E. *Principia Ethica*. New York. Cambridge University Press, 1903

Rand, Ayn, The Virtue of Selfishness: A New Concept of Egoism. New York. Signet, 1964

CHAPTER THREE
NON-CONSEQUENTIALISM

Not all ethical or moral behavior is based on the notion of consequences. Some ethicists believe that consequences should not be the primary concern in determining an act or attitude as moral or immoral. These theories are called Non-Consequentialist. Persons who adhere to this classification of ethical behaviors claim that such behaviors are based on something other than consequences. The Divine Command Theory of ethics is a prime example.

Briefly, the Divine Command Theory claims that moral attitudes and behaviors are established by a 'source' outside of the human being. In Christianity as with other major religions, that source is God or by whatever name that divinity is called. Generally, persons who adhere to the Divine Command Theory rely upon "holy books" and prayer for determining moral behavior. However, other belief systems suggest alternatives. One such system is that of Taoism (pronounced as DOU-is-uhm).

LAO-TZU (SIXTH CENTURY B.C.E.

Lao-Tzu, a contemporary of Confucius, believed that it was a useless endeavor for humankind to attempt to affect change—to make life better for others. For him, Nature was a duality of opposite forces, coming together to work together. This duality is represented by *Yin* and *Yang* and these two opposite forces work in a pattern incomprehensible to most human beings. The thing for the human being to do is to do nothing. That is, let nature take its course. By doing so, you do not obstruct. You do not ask, "What should I do?" but rather you attempt to empty your mind—to let go—to become perfectly still; as still as the stillness of a Chinese jar. In this way, you open yourself to the truth of *The Way*.

Note that the word Nature has been substituted for the word God. Can you see pitfalls in dealing with a moral dilemma if you removed yourself, emptied your mind, and waited for Nature to provide you with the ultimate truth? The final lesson the Taoist would have you learn is to do what you have to do, but don't believe you can make a difference. This doesn't comply with the general attitude of Western culture, but it is an attempt to come to terms with how one should behave.

Another Eastern approach to moral behavior comes from Buddhism.

SIDDHARTHA GUATAMA (BUDDHA) - (563-483 B.C.E.)

Siddhartha Gautama, born into a royal family, renounced the possessions of his position to become a monk. Appalled by the pitiful conditions of his countrymen, Siddhartha determined to find a better way. After a period of depriving himself, he came to realize that such asceticism did not produce solutions or answers.

As the story goes, Siddhartha found his *enlightenment* while sitting under a Bodhi or Bo-tree (a fig tree). After which he was called Buddha (the enlightened one). He set forth the *Four Noble Truths*. Craving, please note, includes wealth, power, position, and all the other material goods that humankind surrounds itself, but not life itself.

Life is full of suffering
Suffering is caused by craving
If craving ceases, suffering will cease
The way to stop craving is to follow the Eightfold Path

The Eightfold Path provides a way to eliminate suffering. The eight pieces of advice are summarized below. Three are stated as "never" or as "don't."

Right Belief Truth is the proper guide of man;

Right Resolve to be calm at all times and not harm any living creature,

Right Speech is to never lie, slander, or use foul language.

Right Behavior is to never steal, kill, or do anything you might regret or be ashamed of,

Right Occupation is to never consider an occupation that might be bad,

Right Effort is to always strive for that which is good and avoid evil,

Right Contemplation is to think on the Noble Truths in calmness and Detachment

Right Concentration will lead to the path of perfect peace.

As in Christianity, the Buddhists have commandments, which prescribe behavior, conduct, and attitude. These Commandments are:

Do not destroy life.

Do not take what is not given to you.

Do not commit adultery.

Tell no lies and deceive no one.

Do not become intoxicated.

Eat temperately and not at all in the afternoon.

Do not watch dancing, nor listen to singing or plays.

Wear no garlands, perfumes or any adornments.

Sleep not in luxurious beds.

Accept no gold or silver.

According to the Buddhist's belief system, all you need to do is follow these steps and you will reach a point of no suffering. Consequently, moral dilemmas will not exist.

In Western culture, non-consequentialism has two distinct divisions: *Rule non-consequentialism* and *Act-non-consequentialism.* Act non-consequentialism revolves around the idea that there are no general moral rules. There are only particular actions and situations about which generalizations cannot be made. Sounds wonderful, doesn't it?

Imagine no rules to obey or to tell you what you ought to do, or to tell you have to behave. How, then are moral decisions made if there are no rules to function as guides? How do you tell right from wrong; good from bad? One approach to making decisions about moral issues is based on *Intuition*.

Intuition is the act of knowing or sensing without the use of rational processes. It is immediate cognition. It is based on what you believe and feel to be so. In terms of morality, it refers to what you believe or feel to be right or wrong. The idea of Intuitionism is highly individualistic in its approach to ethical behavior in that it does not apply to rules based on universality. Frank Sinatra's song, "My Way" exemplifies this approach. Perhaps you have had someone say to you, "If it feels right, do it. It's up to you." But what if your feelings on any given day are different from another given day? Then what do you do?

Intuitionism is accepted because people believe any well-meaning person has a sense of right and wrong and will act accordingly. Do you think serial killers have such a sense? The advocates of Intuitionism also claim that reasoning is used only to confirm what has been intuited. And then, there is the ever-present possibility that your reasoning is wrong. In that situation, what must you rely upon? The answer is intuition.

Criticism of Intuitionism reflects a current attitude about the word intuition itself. It now means a hunch or a guess and lacks credibility. The most striking argument against Intuitionism as a basis for making moral decisions is that there is no absolute proof that you have an innate set of moral rules against which you might judge your actions.[14] What about a person who lacks intuitive skills? Is that person considered immoral because there is no basis for moral decision-making? Or does that individual base moral behavior and decisions on something else?

One of the significant problems of Act non-consequentialism is feelings differ from person to person. What you feel may not be what I feel. Therefore, how are we to resolve any moral differences we might have? All we end up doing is saying that we disagree with each other's feelings. How can anyone know what he or she feels at any given moment is morally right?

Is there another basis other than Intuitionism for making moral judgments within the classification of non-consequentialism? Yes, there are. Two of these, and perhaps two of the more famous, are Immanuel Kant's "Duty Ethics" and W.D. Ross' "Prima Facie Duties." Both of these philosophers have a significant influence on Western moral thought.

Kant's theory, remember, insists that duty is the determiner of moral behavior. If you do not act out of duty, you are not acting morally. The traditional name for this theory is *Deontological* from Greek, *deon* meaning doing what you are supposed to do. It is insisting on doing what you are supposed to do that makes Kant an absolutist. He also insists that moral rules must be applicable universally. This earns him the classification of being a universalist. For now, an absolutist is one who insists that there is only one way to do something and a universalist insists that it apply to everyone in the world. W.D. Ross disagreeing with Kant's absolutism does agree that there are, however, certain duties, **prima facie duties**, that should be followed. What he suggests is an improvement on Kant in that he allows you to choose which duties take priority. Both have their critics.

How do you know if your intentions are good? This is Kant's basic question in his study of ethics. To find out if your intentions are good, Kant wants you to answer another question: "Can your intentions be made into a general (universal) rule for everyone? What this means is your intentions **must** conform to rational principles. So far, so good, but what then, causes you to have moral conflicts? According to Kant, your moral conflicts are caused by our inclinations because they do not always reflect your duties. Karl Marx said it best when he wrote, "The road to hell is paved with good intentions." The road of conflict then is your struggle between your desires and what you are supposed to do. This leads to major criticism of Duty Ethics.

Certainly one of the major criticisms of Kant's ethical theory is that it does not establish for you which rules are morally valid. A rule, according to Kant, to be morally valid, should be universalizable and it should be consistent. Consider the following: One should not help those in need. Can this be made into a rule that is universal and consistent? Even though most people would question such an idea, it can be universalized and it's consistent.

Another criticism of Kant's ethical theory involves his idea called *reversibility criterion.*[15] It is weak. Such a proposal infers the idea of consequences. If an act produces, bad consequences don't do it. The idea itself is inconsistent. Further, Kant in his absolutism leaves no room for exception or distinctions between qualified and unqualified rules. Finally, Kant does not explain what you are to do when your inclinations and duties are the same. If for example, you are inclined not to steal, a tendency that accommodates Kant's rule "do not steal," and one which he says is your duty to obey, does this mean that since you are not inclined to steal you are not a moral person because the duty of not stealing is not pulling you away from your inclinations? Or, what if you are a person inclined to do good, but felt no sense of duty to do so? Are you less of a moral person than one who says it is a duty to do good? Hardly!

The primary argument against Kant's ethics is that it does not allow exceptions—what might be called mitigating circumstances. If this were true, wouldn't many persons that have been found not guilty of certain crimes now be found guilty? Our current legal system would need a massive overhauling.

W.D. Ross rejects the claim that there is one thing of intrinsic value—duty. Further, Ross claims that an act may actually fall under any number of different rules at once; not just a single rule or duty as Kant would have you believe. However, his "prima facie duties" obligate you. Ordinarily, they impose a moral obligation that you must meet. For Ross, an **actual duty** is any action that you ought to perform after you have concerned or weighed all the prima facie duties involved.

Like Kant, W.D. Ross and his "prima facie duties" does not escape criticism. The fundamental criticism is posed by the question, "how are you to decide which duties are indeed **first** duties? Second, "how are you to choose the correct prima facie duty when it conflicts with another? In other words, Ross does not provide you any guidance in making such choices. Finally, Ross bases his selection on intuition in that he presents no logic or rationale to justify any of the choices.

The prima facie duties Ross lists (fidelity, gratitude, justice, beneficence, self-improvement, non-maleficence, and reparation) are self-evident truths. They are self-evident to anyone who has sufficient mental maturity and who has given them careful consideration. But what if you disagree with these seven duties? What does Ross mean by sufficient mental maturity? Or for that matter, what does he mean by 'careful consideration?' Who determines the level of maturity and the degree of consideration? You? Then there is the fundamental criticism posed by these two questions: 1) how are you to decide which duties are indeed, first duties? 2) how are you to choose the correct prima facie duty when it conflicts with another duty?

Once again, Ross does not provide you with any guidance in making your choices. What he does provide falls far short of sound advice. He says, "The act is one's duty which is in accord with the more stringent prima facie obligation. The act is one's duty that has the greatest balance of prima facie rightness." How are you to know, which is the most stringent duty, and which has a greater balance?

INTERACTIVE EIGHT

Directions:

Read the following scenario and then answer the questions that follow.

The Scenario

You are walking along a city street. As you approach a particular store, you hear shots. A man staggers through the doorway of the shop and collapses on the sidewalk. A second man falls into the open doorway. He is alive. You don't know which one is the 'bad guy'.

The Questions

What do you do? Would you try to help the man that is alive?
 Or would you check on the dead man?

Would you call 911?
Would you run away?

Which philosopher will guide your actions: Kant or Ross? Justify your choice.

SUGGESTED ANSWER TO INTERACTIVE EIGHT

You have several issues. First, you do not know who the shooter is; nor do you know if there is another shooter. There is no indication that the two men are not dead; nor do you know the nature of their wounds. Kant does not allow exceptions. Your best bet is to follow the ethics of Ross. Even though he does not indicate how you are to choose the prima facie duties, you are to follow; there is an underlying implication that one's own life comes first. In the event, there is another shooter and he shoots and kills you or severely wounds you, you cannot be of any help to those on the ground. Your choice is to seek cover and dial 911.

GLOSSARY OF TERMS

Absolutist --- One who believes there are moral rules that are absolute, that is, rules which contain no exception.

Act non-consequentialism --- Claims there are no general moral rules, only particular actions, and situations about which generalizations cannot be made.

Actual duty --- Any action that you ought to perform after you have considered all other prima facie duties.

Deon --- Greek word meaning, "doing what you are supposed to do."

Deontological --- Kant's theory of 'duty ethics' that insists that duty is the determiner of moral behavior, that is, if one does not act out of duty, he or she is not acting morally.

Eightfold Path --- In Buddhism, the outline of behavior necessary to find enlightenment.

Four Noble Truths --- Fundamental statements in Buddhism that indicate the cause of suffering and lead to the Eightfold Path to enlightenment.

Intuition --- The act of knowing or sensing without the use of rational processes.

Non-consequentialism --- Consequences should not be the primary concern in determining an act or attitude as moral or immoral.

Prima facie duties --- Duties which take priority; those which come first over other alternatives.

Reversibility criterion --- Applies the concept of the Gold Rule in reverse order by asking the question, 'would you have others do to you what you would do to them?'

Rule non-consequentialism --- There are general rules that function as the basis for moral decision-making.

Universalist --- One who believes there are universal moral principles that apply to all persons.

SUGGESTED READINGS

Bayles, Michael D. & Kenneth Henley, eds. **Right Conduct: Theories and Applications, 2nd ed**. New York: Random House, 1989.

Eliade, Mircea, **A History of Religious Ideals, Vol 2**. (William R. Trask, trans.) Chicago: University of Chicago Press, 1984.

Hospers, John, **Human Conduct, 2nd ed.** New York: Harcourt, Brace, and World, 1982.

Kant, Immanuel, **Fundamental Principles of Metaphysics of Morals** (H.J. Paton, trans.) New York: Harper & Row, 1957.

Parrinder, Geoffrey, ed. **World Religions from Ancient History to the Present.** New York: Facts on File Publications, 1983.

Paton, Herbert J. The Categorical Imperative: A Study in Kant's Moral Philosophy. Chicago: University of Chicago Press, 1948.

Wright, Robert, The Moral Animal, Why We Are the Way We Are: The New Science of Evolutionary Psychology. New York: Pantheon, 1994

CHAPTER FOUR
ABSOLUTISM AND RELATIVISM

Absolutism and relativism are the two extremes of the ethical pole; both contain strong arguments for adoption. Within these broad descriptive categories, there are divergent theories of moral conduct. For example, **Ethical Absolutism** holds that there is only *one* correct morality. A *moral absolute* is a principle that is universally binding; one that cannot be overridden by another principle. Absolute has several meanings. Among those that have an application to the current discussion are "perfect in quality and no exceptions," "not to be doubted or questioned," and "fixed." A regular dictionary lists other definitions and if the definition is as varied as the dictionary suggests, you can readily see the difficulty in coming to any agreement as to what is morally right or wrong.

The difficulty is compounded when morality is associated with religious beliefs. The morality that is religiously directed is generally absolute. In Christianity, the divine being is called God and His authority is absolute, beyond question. However, another example of ethical absolutism comes from *Utilitarianism.*

Utilitarianism holds to only one ethical absolute principle: "Do that action that maximizes utility." A word of caution is appropriate here. There are absolutist theories that do contain more than one absolute. The ethical theory of Immanuel Kant is such an example. It contains several absolutes, which he called *categorical imperatives*. One of these categorical imperatives states that you are to treat humankind as an end and never merely as a means. (This applies to just one individual as well.) Other theories may have only a few absolutes while others may contain the idea that there is only one correct answer to moral dilemmas.

Morality is by its very nature a set of universal principles—principles that do not make a distinction between cultures, people, or lifestyles. It is morally wrong to kill another human being just for the fun of it, and this is true in all cultures. The absolutist holds there is but one eternally true and valid morality and it applies to all human beings without exception. Simply put, this means that there is not a different set of moral behaviors for South Americans and another for North Americans, and yet another for the French or a set for Catholics while Baptist and Methodists both enjoy different sets of morality. There is but one law. It is absolute, unchangeable, and permanent. The law does not change with time or with condition. The old and famous cliché, when in Rome do as the Romans do" is unacceptable. The same holds true for Los Vegas. Furthermore, just because you think something is right does not make it so. Even Jean-Luc cannot will it with his now famous, "Make it so." The law is because it is. What you or anyone else things makes no difference.

This is powerful and for some of you, it may be frightening. From where did such a concept come?

Most likely ethical absolutism is the direct result of two sources in the Western world: the ancient Greek philosopher, Plato, and the advent of Christianity. American philosopher, Walter Stace claims, "morality was conceived during the Christian dispensation, as issuing from the will of God."[16]

PLATO (427-347 B.C.E.)

Plato argued for the objectivity of moral principles in contrast to those who promulgated morality as a matter of opinion or preference. From his point of view, your actions are right or wrong *absolutely* and *independent* of anyone's opinions, thoughts, or beliefs. They are as absolute as one plus one equals two are. That is true now as you read this, it was true yesterday, and it will be true tomorrow. There are no "ifs, and or buts" about it. The impact of Plato's thoughts on early Christianity cannot be estimated, nevertheless; it has been significant. God's word and laws are absolute, unchanging, and permanent. However, now, it should be noted that Plato believed that moral standards were superior even to God. Goodness, for example, is antecedent to God. According to Platonic thought, God is good if and only if he acts in accordance with the standard of goodness. Note, this is entirely different from the Christian viewpoint. God for Plat was not the present Judeo-Christian view of divinity. Remember, the Greeks of Plato's day were polytheistic.

Plato believed if a person had knowledge of the good life, that person would never act immorally. Plato believed that there was one and only one good life for all men. Philosophers have leveled criticism against Plato, including his own pupil, Aristotle.

ARISTOTLE (384-322 B.C.E.)

Accordingly, Aristotle said, "the proper way for a man to behave in the moral sphere is in accordance with the *mean*." With this came what is now the well-known and famous Golden Mean. There are two other important Aristotelian concepts to be considered:

The good life is a life of happiness.

Men ought to behave so as to achieve happiness.

Happiness depends on the individual; that is, what makes one person happy may not be sufficient to make another person happy. Aristotle said that you should strive for the *mean*. The mean is a keyword in Aristotle's ethics, and it does not refer to average, but rather it refers to any point between. For example, if you eat a "quarter pounder" and still feel hungry, Aristotle suggests you eat another. If at that point you feel stuffed, then does it imply the next time you eat only one and a half quarter pounders? Not necessarily. You may choose to eat less or more. The Golden Mean is the point at which you are satisfied, comfortable, and happy. Perhaps you had to eat one, and only a small part of a second "quarter pounder" to achieve this state. In other words, in order to find your Golden Mean, you must experiment using the trial-and-error approach. You cannot determine beforehand what will make you happy by reasoning alone. What this means for your moral behavior is that there are various correct ways of living for different people. What may be good for you may or may not be good for someone else. For you to achieve happiness, you must act *moderately,* and you must act in such a way as to bring about the bean between extremes. A good action then is one that is not excessive or one that is lacking. Courage, for example, is the mean between rashness and cowardice. All of this makes Aristotle a **relativist**.

The battle lines between absolutism and relativism have been drawn. At some point, you have heard words such as fundamentalist, conservative, liberal, ultraconservative, right-wing, and or left-wing. One group accuses the other of lacking "good morals," and the other retorts with such slogans as "Get real!" Such charges and counter-charges become especially apparent during heated political issues and campaigns or during a perceived national crisis. The modern relativist expresses his views through such slogans as "If it feels good, do it" or "Do your own thing." In liberal Christianity, relativism is expressed by such statements "as long as you fulfill the commandment of love, then anything goes." Can you see this applied to a situation in which one spouse kills the other because one is suffering, and the killing is done because of the love the kill as for the other? Who is to say what love is?

As with absolute, the word relative has its different meanings, including such words as comparative, flexible, indefinite, provisional, conditional, and ancillary. Further analysis of these words reveals an inherent idea cropping up at the surface —that idea being—morals are temporary. What is right within one group may be utterly abhorrent to members of another group. What may be held morally correct may not be held in another epoch. The suggestion here is that morals vary from culture to culture. A person who believes this is called a *cultural relativist.* Those philosophers who came after the Kantian revolution in philosophy rushed pell-mell into relativism with such enthusiasm that they could not find publishers quick enough. One philosopher, Friedrich Schelling, for example, was producing a new system yearly. Another giant of philosophy emerging during this period of "new ideas" was Georg Wilhelm Friedrich Hegel. Hegel admonished his fellow things to "stop talking about true and false philosophies, and true and false religions, political systems, societies, scientific theories, and values." For Hegel, they were only different forms of "consciousness" and none was better the exclusion of others. Friedrich Nietzsche claimed there could be as many equally "true or false" views as there were creative people and societies.

FRIEDRICH NIETZSCHE (1844-1900)

Friedrich Nietzsche was born near Leipzig, Germany. His father, a minister, died when Nietzsche was very young, leaving him to be brought up by a bevy of women: his mother, grandmother, sister, and two maiden aunts.

After leaving the University of Bonn where he was a theology student, Nietzsche went to the University of Leipzig. He was viewed as a brilliant student in classical philology and even before completing his doctorate requirements, he was offered a position as professor of philology at the University of Basel in Switzerland. Without taking his examinations, he was awarded his doctorate by the University of Leipzig when he was twenty-four years old. His first book, The Birth of Tragedy[17] was published in 1872.

Nietzsche rejected any systematic approach to the human being. His very intense personalism placed humankind as the only true object of philosophy. He called for a transformation and at the center of this transformation was his concept of *Übermensch* or Overman[18] who was free to create new values. Universal morality had to be rejected because, according to Nietzsche, it destroyed the individual's freedom to act in accordance with his own creative insights. The notion of universal morality, forcing everyone to behave in the same way, was a dark cloud — a blight upon humankind—that Nietzsche felt had to be dispersed.Dividing morality into *master morality* and *slave morality* set the stage for Nietzsche's renunciation of God. His master morality stresses independence, self-approbation, and personal action based on strength or power. Slave morality, on the other hand, is equated to what is now called herd mentality. The salve moralist exhibits insecurity, lack of self-confidence, and bases action ion resentment, and an emphasis on humility and patience. For Nietzsche, Christianity inhibited creativity, freedom, independence, and encouraged blind obedience. Proclaiming, "God is dead," [19] Nietzsche sent challenge ricocheting throughout Europe: the master moralist creates his own values and is beholding to no one for those values. His morality is one of self-glorification and such a man is called a noble man for he is the determiner of values; the one who passes judgment.

In The Genealogy of Morals, Nietzsche declares, "Life itself is essential assimilation, injury, violation of the foreign and the weaker, suppression, hardness, the forcing of one's form upon something else, ingestion and exploitation." Do you think a person who practices a mast morality would stop and give help to someone in need because he felt obligated to help his fellow human being? The master moralist would stop and render help to the unfortunate but not out of a sense of duty, beneficence, or because he felt, he was his brother's keeper. He would give help based on an impulse generated by an abundance of power, in this case, the power to make the unfortunate person obligated to him.

Because Nietzsche believed each person creates his or her own morality and values such a belief identifies him as a relativist. The question now becomes what a cultural relativist believes.

The cultural relativist believes that any notion of universal moral truth is a myth. The claim is that customs in different cultures is all that exists. Custom means the practice of a group of people in a particular region. There is no indication as to the rightness or wrongness of the acts considered custom. The cultural relativist claims that to make such judgments implies that you have an independent standard of rightness or wrongness by which you make your moral judgments. For the cultural relativist, there is no such thing as an independent standard because all standards, whatever they may be, are bound to the culture in which they exist and are therefore different. What then, do the cultural relativists believe?

The cultural relativists make the following six claims:

Different societies have different moral codes

An objective standard that can be used to judge once societal code as being better than another does not exist

The moral code of American society has no special status; it is only one among many

There are no moral truths that apply to all people at all times

Any given society determines what is right or wrong within its moral code.

An attitude of tolerance is preferable to trying to judge the conduct of others.

CASE STUDY 1.5 - (DAVID & GEORGE)

Background Data

David Ruppert is the CEO and owner of a manufacturing company. He has clawed his way up, making his business a success. He demands 110% of his employees and 125% of himself. He measures his success in terms of net profits. To increase that success he is attempting to buy up a smaller company in a nearby city. Negotiations have stalled for several weeks and he has decided to take charge of the negotiations personally.

The Scenario

David is driving to Richfield, a two-hour drive north of his present location. He has decided to drive to gain some additional time to review his pitch. He felt he always did better thinking when he was behind the wheel of his BMW.

Because of a problem with his company's computers, David has gotten a later start than he had planned. A drizzle has made the driving unpleasant and has forced him to slow down. He calls ahead to George Wainright, the owner of the company he is trying to buy to tell him he is running late. Wainright doesn't answer the phone.

"Typical," David muttered to himself. "Never takes care of business. Always out of the office. No wonder the company is in trouble."

A car sped past him going at an excessive speed. The roads were slippery because it had not rained for several weeks. The rain made the oil on the road dangerously slippery.

"Idiot," David muttered.

He was about to say something more when he realized a set of headlights were headed right at him. He jerked the steering wheel to the left to avoid a head-on collision. The on-coming car careened off the road, smashing through a guardrail. David eased his BMW off the road, backed up and got out his car to see if anyone was hurt.

As David approached the wreck, the car burst into flames. He could see a body slumped against the partially opened door. He grabbed the body and pulled, dragged the man away from the burning car. The man was bleeding profusely from a large gash in his neck. Booze filled the air. David raced back to his car, grabbed a first aid kit, flares, and his cell phone.

"How do you apply a tourniquet to a person's throat? You don't," he heard himself say.

He looked at the man. It was George Wainright.

"Don't you dare die! Have you signed the papers? Answer me."

David grabbed his cell phone. He looked at it. "Might be easier to deal with his wife," he thought. "Naw."

He dialed 911 and the voice at the other end told him what to do until help arrived.

David followed the ambulance to a hospital. Two hours later, he was sitting beside Wainright's bed.

"I owe you my life," Wainright whispered.

"Yeah, and a company, too," David replied.

INTERACTIVE NINE

Directions:

Answer each of these questions.

What is the primary moral issue? What makes it a moral issue?

What is the primary moral principle?

What is David's attitude? How is this attitude shown in the scenario?

How could David's actions and attitude be justified?

What moral system is reflected by David?

The significant question is what is the right way? American sociologist, William Graham Sumner put the answer to this question this way:

The "right" way is the way, which the ancestors used and which had been handed down. The tradition is its own warrant. It is not held subject to verification by experience. The notion of right is in the folkways. It is not outside of them, of independent origin, and brought to test them. In the folkways, whatever is, is right. This is because they are traditional, and therefore, contain in themselves the authority of the ancestral ghosts. When we come to the folkways we are at the end of our analysis [of morals].[20]

Just suppose for a moment, you accept this notion of "whatever is, is right." What would be some consequences? If this were the accepted behavior, you would not be in a position to level any criticism against any of the horrors going on around the world. Those who preach hate and bigotry would go unchallenged.

Can you decide whether actions are right or wrong by just checking the standards of society? According to the cultural relativist, all you would have to do is ask if the intended action(s) are in accordance with the code of your society. If it is, then you have nothing to worry about. After all, isn't this why we hire ministers, priests, rabbis? Isn't that why you put black-robed people on a bench (judges) or in blue uniforms (police officers)? To let you know what is right action.

It is this that disturbs some people—this

being told. Under cultural relativism, you are not allowed to criticize because it implies making judgments about your culture. Since you are not supposed to judge other cultures, judging your own would be incongruous. How can you say progress has been made? How can you ever say that any moral improvement has been achieved? Women's rights serve as a good example. During the early part of the last century, women were not held in high esteem. They could not vote or hold public office. In many states, a single woman could not inherit property. The property had to be placed under the management of an "older" male relative. If a woman should dare to seek a divorce, she lost her home, her security, and her children. The house, its furnishings, and any children were the property of the husband. Women were not expected to be employed outside of the home. Few careers were open to women. Typists were men. Today, women in many countries around the world do not have the rights American women enjoy. If cultural relativism is correct, you probably would not think of the rights now held by women as progress. Why? To say that women have made progress is to make a judgment that present-day society is better than the past society. This is transcultural judgment and is, according to the cultural relativist, not permissible.

If all of this is true, what is there about ethical relativism that makes it attractive? Lawrence M. Hinman in *Ethics: A Pluralistic Approach to Moral Theory* suggests the following three reasons for the attractiveness of ethical relativism.

Ethical relativism encourages moral tolerance and understanding,

Some people believe that everything is relative, and for them, ethical relativism is just a corollary of a more generalized relativism they hold about all beliefs,

Many times human beings feel they do not have the right to make moral judgments about other human beings.

Of course, moral tolerance and understanding is an attitude in keeping with a democratic society. It seems to suggest an attitude of "live and let live."

CHAPTER FIVE
RIGHTS, JUSTICE, & EQUALITY

You have rights by the mere fact that you exist!

Such rights are thought to exist universally. The United States Constitution guarantees you certain "unalienable rights. What exactly does that mean? It means there are certain rights that you cannot have taken away from you, and you cannot give them away without due process. The belief that you have these certain unalienable rights forms the basis for equal treatment under the law. Further, these rights form the basis for claims against another individual, against employers, governments, and even a whole society. Rights involve citizens, non-citizens, spouses, children, parents, animals, environment, employment, education, and nations. Individual rights have not always been held sacrosanct. Humankind's struggle for rights has bloodied rivers and filled fields with the dead. That struggle continues as civilizations attempt to define and clarify that which constitutes rights. Traditionally, in the United States, Americans refer to the "Bill of Rights" which includes the "freedoms" of speech, press, and religion. This is not the worldview. Human beings, the world over continue to struggle for the fundamental rights that define human dignity. The United States still struggles with issues of race, ethnicity, and economic disparity.

There are two kinds of law, prescriptive and descriptive. ***Prescriptive law*** refers to those social rules that regulate your behavior; the customs and mores of the culture to which you belong.[21] Most states in the United States require a marriage license if you want legal recognition for your union. The battle over what constitutes a marriage still rages on despite the number of states now legally accepting gay marriage. Abortion and the rights of a woman to control her own body are other examples of Prescriptive Law.

Descriptive law, on the other hand, describes what actually happens under certain conditions; for example, scientific laws would describe the reaction when atoms collide. In ethics, the term ***natural law*** is used to mean a set of prescriptive rules of conduct that are not exclusively prescribed within any given culture for the regulation of its own social life, but rather, apply to all human beings and are bound to all human beings.

Conceptually the idea of natural laws is quite old in that it can be traced back to the early Greeks of the fourth century B.C. E. for its origins. More accurately, it may be traced back to the early Sumerians or Egyptians; however, it was Aristotle who provided an account of human nature that continues to influence Western thinking. His central thought is that each kind of thing has a purpose, *toles*, as it is called in Greek.

ARISTOTLE (384-322 B.C.E.)

Aristotle was born in the city of Stagira in Thrace. Because he was the son of a physician at the court of Macedon, it has been suggested that he probably trained in the medical arts; however, at eighteen he went to Athens to complete his education. There he entered Plato's Academy and remained for twenty years, and then, only leaving upon Plato's death in 348 B.C.E. He traveled for nearly a decade, taught Alexander the Great, son of Philip of Macedon, and finally returned to Athens in 335/334 B.C. E. where he opened his own school, the Lyceum.

When the Athenians revolted against the rule of Macedon, they attached Aristotle because of his close ties with the Macedonian Court. He left Athens in 323. Aristotle's far-ranging interests included logic, physics, political science, astronomy, biology, psychology, aesthetics, and ethics.

According to Aristotle's *teleology*, the goal of each thing is to act in accordance with its distinctive characteristics that are common to all of its kind. In his *Nichomachean Ethics*, named after his son, Aristotle lists rationality as the distinctive characteristic of human nature; rational activity then becomes the proper mode of behavior for human beings. He then adds right conduct, which is to have as its aim human happiness—found in human activity that expresses its distinctive characteristics of rationality. Further, this activity must involve sufficient external goods to meet human emotional physical needs. His lists include friends, family, healthy, and money. Aristotle also claimed that it made no difference whether the activities themselves were the end actions or something else apart from those activities.

Not everyone agreed with this position, the *Stoics* for example. Even though the Stoics accepted the Aristotelian concept of rationality, they maintained that the principle of right conduct involved following nature rather than convention or custom. This does not mean that they would have you pursue every whim or desire that you may have; quite to the contrary, the Stoics downplayed the importance of external goods and devalued human emotion.

The Natural Law Theory, for all practical purposes, involves the natural abilities and inclinations of human beings. Its fundamental principle is that of right conduct and the avoidance of evil or bad conduct. As you have seen, what constitutes the good varies from culture to culture and from epoch to epoch. Yet, there are universal human goods. These include life itself, health, and procreation, rearing of the young, interpersonal relationships, knowledge, and truth. [22] The American guarantee of "life, liberty, and the pursuit of happiness" summarizes this point very nicely.

Some questions for your consideration. Do you have the right to read and view what you wish? Do you have the right to yell "fire" at a crowded concert when there is no fire? Do you have the right not to be sexually propositioned? Can you, if you want, enjoy pornography? Is there a difference between yelling "fire" at a crowded concert and telling your friend there is a bug in his or her soup? Just because procreation is a human right, does it mean a woman must have a child if her husband wants her to? Does a wife have the right to expect and to receive her husband's estate upon his death? Do you have the right to run around nude in your own home? Do you have the right to live in a dwelling that is not subjected to electronic surveillance? As a human being living in a free society, what are your expectations?

What does it mean to have a right? To have a right implies that you are in a position to demand it as your due. What then, are the characteristics and functions of rights? First, rights exist in what is called the *realm of entitlements*. The issue of entitlements has occupied a good deal of the political world as governments struggle with the whole gambit of social issues.

Entitlement means that you are authorized; you do not need the consent of another. You are empowered! Further, because rights are yours inherently, you are under no obligation to make other relevant considerations, even though it might, in the end, be to your best advantage. If something is your right, you may cite that as your justification for a particular behavior. The claim of a right calls attention to a wrong that has been perpetrated against you. Life is a right; driving an automobile is a privilege and as such, it may be revoked. Rights function as a delineation of certain expectations.

You have a right to be held free from harm by another individual. You have the expectation of going about your affairs free from the threat of being mugged, raped, or killed. This may not be the case, but it is the fundamental expectation. Do you think modern Americans no longer hold this expectation? Have Americans given up and surrendered to street gangs, rapists, murderers, and or muggers. Do young men and women at college have to accept a drug and rape culture? Do schoolchildren now have to accept being bullied as a part of their daily lives?

CHARACTERISTICS OF A HUMAN RIGHT

It must be possessed by all human beings and only human beings.
It must be possessed equally by all human beings.
Rights one has by virtue of status, position, or relationship are not viewed as human rights, and
The right must be assertable.

Richard Wasserstrom's "Rights, Human Rights, and Racial Discrimination"[23] lists four identifying characteristics of a human right. Pause and think about each of the items on Wasserstrom's list. It becomes quite evident that there is an implication that human rights are absolute, that is, there are no exceptions. Human rights are absolute in that they are possessed equally without any special qualifiers by all human beings. Further, note that Wasserstrom is not implying that there are any conditions under which such rights may be overridden. A person convicted of a serious crime against society and is sentenced to life in prison loses his or her rights to vote, to hold public office, and to procreate. [Some prisons now allow conjugal visits.]

CASE STUDY 1.6 - (CUSTODY BATTLE)

Background Data[24]

Two Native American Indian girls of mixed blood, ages ten and eight, have been living with their white aunt and uncle for two years. Bill, the father, a salesman for a national manufacturer of heavy industrial equipment is killed in a fiery plane crash in Colorado while showing a potential client the Grand Canyon. Bill and his wife, Anna, had separated. She has returned to her family on the reservation.

The Scenario

In his will, Bill had left instructions that his two daughters should be raised by his family, specifically his brother Ed and his wife, Betty. They lived in a comfortable suburban home, close to their church and school. They have a five-year-old son of their own, are good parents, and are willing to raise their nieces.

Anna, Bill's estranged wife has sued for custody of her children and has demanded the girls be turned over to her.

Ed and Betty are concerned about the kind of life the girls will have on the reservation since they are of mixed blood. They also have concerns about the quality of education, health care, and the general well-being of the girls. At best, they claim, such care would be minimal.

Bill has left a considerable amount of money from an insurance policy to the girls. It has been set up as a trust fund for them. Ed and Betty are concerned that Anna will not use the money wisely for the benefit of the girls, especially since she is dating, drinking, and drugging again—the cause of the breakup of her marriage and Bill's filing for divorce. Ed and Betty question whether Anna would be a responsible parent. They have challenged her rights as a mother and have gone to court to be appointed permanent guardians of the two girls.

It has been two and a half years since Bill's tragic death and Anna has not seen her two daughters during that time. Now that she has found out that there is a trust fund for the girls, she wants them back with control of the trust. She claims, as their mother, she has a legal right to her children. Further, she claims she has stopped drinking and drugging. Her Native American parents and friends support her. They claim she will not be raising the girls alone. Homes on the reservation are a part of an extended family, which provides a wide-range safety net for the girls.

The girls do not want to leave Ed and Betty and go and live in a strange place with people they do not know.

INTERACTIVE TEN

Directions:

Using the background data and the scenario above, create an appropriate ending of your won.

You may use dialogue, have the action take place before a judge, or between the parties involved with a family counselor.

Once you have created your ending and written it out, answer the following questions.

What is the primary moral issue?

What is the primary moral principle?

What is the primary moral theory involved?

What "rights" are involved? Whose are they?

Do you consider these "rights" to be absolute? Explain your answer by citing the reasons for your choice.

One of the things highly valued in Western Culture is the right to privacy. As an idea, privacy is a relatively late development in human history. With the advent of the printing press and the creation of an audience for the printed word, people found they needed a quiet place free from intrusion to read. Over the years, privacy became important. But is it an unalienable right? Certainly, in today's culture, it is assumed. Siblings squabble over the privacy of their bedrooms. Parents put their bedrooms off-limits to their children. Children do not want their rooms searched by their parents. They do not want their laptops, iPads, and iPhones, checked by their parents. Children are affronted by such parental actions. Are students' school lockers and backpacks free from search? If they aren't, is that a rights violation?

Homes, places of business, churches, synagogues, and mosques are all free from unauthorized search. A person's body cannot be searched without just cause and due process. That seems to be changing in today's unsettled world. A woman or a man who has been raped has had their rights to privacy violated.

Do you have the right to do whatever you wish in your privacy? Can you use illegal drugs and claim exemption from the law because you do so in the privacy of your home? Can you use the privacy of your home to plot, by force, to overthrow the United States Government? Or plot to blow up a public place? Obviously, you cannot. Nor can you use the privacy of your home to plot the maiming or death of another individual. As much as you abhor the invasion of your privacy, it is not sacred—anywhere!

The following case study illustrates the complexity of the right to privacy issue.

CASE STUDY 1.7 (GINA)

Background Data

Gina, a senior at Holt High School, has been absent from school quite a few times; her grades have fallen and she has become moody. Mr. Sharp, her English teacher, has noticed that Gina's physical appearance has changed from being neat to sloppy, and her hair is unkempt. Gina frequently asks to leave her class to go to the restroom. When she returns she appears passive and her pupils are dilated.

The Scenario

The class had been studying Oedipus. Mr. Sharp called upon Gina to answer a question. She became upset and accused him of always picking on her. Yelling obscenities at him, she ran from the classroom.

Mr. Sharp wrote a quick note to the school's principal in which he stated he thought Gina was under the influence of drugs and asked that he send the security to locate her. He handed the note to another student to deliver the note to the office. On the way to the office, the student opened the note and read it.

After receiving the note, the principal and a security guard went to Mr. Sharp's classroom. While the three of them were talking outside of the classroom, the student who read the note told another student about its contents.

The principal and the security guard went to Gina's locker. Unlocking it with a master key, they found two small plastic bags containing what appeared to be crack cocaine. Returning to his office, the principal, using an intercom, called Gina to the office. By this time, many students knew about the contents of Mr. Sharp's note and assumed Gina was in serious trouble.

Gina's mother was called to come to the school and pick her up because her daughter had been suspended until the school's investigation was completed.

The substance in Gina's locker was crack and she was suspended from school for the rest of the year.

Gina sued the school principal, the security guard, Mr. Sharp, and the Board of Education claiming her right to privacy had been violated when they searched her locker. She also claimed her right to confidentiality had been violated when Mr. Sharp sent the note to the principal without it being sealed.

Discussion of the case

Did the school principal, security guard, and Mr. Sharp violate Gina's right to privacy? Were her other rights violated? Is a student's locker held inviolate without a search warrant? Did Mr. Sharp behave in an unethical way when he sent the unsealed note to the principal? Did the student who read the note and then told of its content behave in an unethical manner?

The school board maintained that the locker belonged to the school district. It further claimed the locker was only loaned to Gina for her use during the school year. To demonstrate a lack of permanence the attorney for the school board pointed out that each year students were assigned different lockers.

The court ruled that since the school district owned the locker it was not violating Gina's privacy by unlocking and searching its contents. Further, there was no evidence to suggest that Mr. Sharp's behavior was malicious in intent when he sent the note by a student to the principal. The judge also noted that even though Mr. Sharp may have used poor judgment, he had not violated Gina's right to confidentiality.

INTERACTIVE ELEVEN

Answer each of the following questions.

Do you think Gina's rights were violated? On what basis do you make this judgment?

What is the primary moral issue in this scenario?

3. Do you think Gina's use of obscene language should have been brought up during the court procedures? Why? Why not?

4. Do you think Gina's outburst should have been used against her since it was disruptive to the class?

5. If you were the teacher, how would you respond to such an outburst? If you were a fellow student, how would you react?

Expectations of American Citizens

One will be paid for hard work.

Those who do bad things will be punished.

That which one has worked for will not be seized and taken away by the government.

Those in need will be given help.

Closely allied with the issue of rights is the question of justice. *Justice* may be defined as "conformity to moral rightness in action and attitude." It also involves fair treatment and reward in accordance with honor, standards, or law. Edmund Burke, an eighteenth-century British statesman, wrote, "Justice is itself the great standing policy of civil society, and any eminent departure from it, under any circumstance., lies under the suspicion of being no policy at all." But what does "standing policy" entail? Citizens of the United States view themselves as having certain expectations. Of these, only four are listed here. Most likely, you can think of others that should be included. However, the point here is the very expectations that lead to problems.

What happens when not all of these expectations are met? Justice's concern is with prioritizing these expectations and with bringing about a balance between often-conflicting priorities. Justice is never easy. The hope is that it is tempered with understanding, compassion, and mercy. Laws are created to help insure that justice is exactly that—justice!

Within the concept of justice is the idea of *equality*, which is especially important to Americans. Americans tend to like the idea that "all men are created equal." At least, that is the view presented to the public and the world. The sexist language has been changed from "men" to human beings as our culture struggles with equal treatment of women, homosexuals, disadvantaged, and minorities. As a culture, diverse[25] in color, ethnic origins, and religious beliefs, America must also recognize that not everyone is equal. Not everyone weighs the same, runs the same mile, or jumps as high. Nor does everyone have the same kind of intelligence or abilities. Equality becomes important as a legal concept; that is, the laws of the land do not recognize rank, position, privilege, and or gender as granting special or exceptional treatment. Can you think of an exception to this? Are children, as a rule, executed in this country for committing premeditated murder? Does trying young persons as "adults" suggest a shift in the national social values when it comes to justice? Has the paradigm of justice changed in the United States? If so, is this shift good or bad?

One of the more bizarre cases in which justice is the issue comes from the world of literature, William Shakespeare's ***The Merchant of Venice***. Portia, dressed as the man Balthasar, and pretending to be a lawyer, makes the following impassioned plea for mercy and justice before a Viennese court of justice;

> The quality of mercy is not strain'd;
> It droppeth as the gentle rain from the heaven
> Upon the place beneath: it is twice blest;
> It blesseth him that gives, and him that takes:
> Tis mightiest in the mightiest: it becomes
> The throned monarch better than his crown;
> His scepter shows the force of temporal power,
> The attribute to awe and majesty,
> Wherein doth sit the dread and fear of kings;
> But mercy is above this sceptered sway;
> It is enthroned in the hearts of kings,
> It is an attribute of God himself,
> And earthly power doth then show likest God's
> When mercy's seasons justice.[26]

INTERACTIVE TWELVE
Directions:

This activity has three parts. First, read the Fourth Act of Shakespeare's *The Merchant of Venice* second read the essay "The Hypocrisy of Mercy is Not Strange" which follows these directions. Third, complete the assignment at the end of the essay.

The Hypocrisy of Mercy is Not Strange

Balthasar, that ringer who is really Portia, has a brand of mercy all her own. And it is surely strained. Anyone as hypocritical as she and her Christian friends would have to strain to like Atlas holding the world before they could show one scruple of that precious virtue—justice tempered with mercy. Like a gentle rain mercy may droppeth, but what but when the fair Portia is the one seeding the rain clouds.

A Christian must be merciful! The Bible says it and the lawyer (Portia) did praise it. Yet, when our dissembling Portia slyly got Shylock by his throat, did she follow her preachments? Was she merciful? No, a thousand times no. She out-Shylocked with her bitter triumph. Justice? He had cried for his bond; so she cried for his death or ruination only just having finished her speech about the quality of mercy.

Consider Shylock's life. What mattered most to him? His means of livelihood, his beautiful daughter, and his religious beliefs. Now he has none of these. His money is gone; he has none to lend, thus no job. Thanks to the mercy of Portia. His daughter has run off with his treasure. Thanks to Lorenzo, Portia's caretaker. Gone also is his religion, which he had always lived by and quoted from. All thanks to merciful Portia. Praise be to Portia. Merci, grande merci; Merciful Portia.

To condemn Shylock for seeking revenge is only to doubly damn Portia in the same breath for the same act. To say that the Jew tricked Antonio is again only to repeat that Shylock, in turn, was tricked by Portia. However, there is a difference. Shylock openly admitted his motives in court. Portia, on the other hand, had such high oral ideals and yet such low moral ideals. If this be mercy that she practices, then woe be to Bassanio if he ever finds fair Portia in an unmerciful mood. Fair Portia indeed—in the color of her hair only!

ASSIGNMENT

Respond to the essay, The Hypocrisy of Mercy is Not Strange by agreeing or disagreeing with its underlying concept. Is Portia hypocritical? What justice does she demand? What is the idea of justice presented in the essay? Write out your answers.

INTERACTIVE THIRTEEN

Directions:

Select one of the two following quotations. In a short essay, agree or disagree with the quotation of your choice.

Quotation One:
Ambrose Bierce states, "Justice is a commodity which in a more or less adulterated condition in the State sells to the citizen as a reward for his allegiance, taxes, and personal service."

Quotation Two:
Voltaire wrote, "The sentiment of justice is so rational and so universally acquired by all mankind that it seems to be independent of all law, all party, and all religion."

***

Ethicists often divide rights into three types even though some create a larger division.
Natural rights
Moral rights
Legal rights

Natural rights are defined, generally, as those belonging to human beings simply because they are human beings. Over the years, ethical theorists have attempted to establish a firm basis for the claim that human beings have certain natural rights. Most of these attempts center around four areas:

Human rights are self-evident

Human rights are granted by God

Human rights are based on natural law, and

Human rights are based on the characteristics of the individual.

The framers of the American Declaration of Independence used the term *unalienable* to describe rights. What is implied here is that human rights exist—period. Such an attitude is an inherent part of the American national character. Americans believe that their rights are self-evident. But this, the advocates of the self-evident concept of rights believe that human rights are so obvious that it would unthinkable to question their existence. Among these self-evident rights are the right to life, liberty, and the pursuit of happiness. Does history demonstrate the validity of such a notion of human rights? Unfortunately, it does not. There are still many struggles for these inherent rights to be applied to all members of the American society.

How is the phrase, "the pursuit of happiness" to be defined? Can it be used to justify the use of illegal drugs? Hardly! Such an application has not been in the purview of the courts or is there any written evidence that it was ever the intention of the framers of the Declaration.

The notion of *human rights are given by God* and be taken away only by God is based, of course upon Christian religious beliefs. The obvious right is that of life. And strong support comes from that conviction. If a man and woman cannot procreate, it is said to be God's will; that is, their right to produce their own kind has been denied by God. Is it the reason why a child is stillborn? Has God denied it the right to life, liberty, and the pursuit of happiness? Tough questions and they are raised by ethicists, philosophers, and religious thinkers alike. Thornton Wilder in *The Bridge of San Luis Rey* explores the issue of why certain persons had their lives suddenly ended; denied the right to life.

The *natural law* advocates claim human rights re a part of the natural order of the universe and that order is by nature good. Desmond Morris in his *The Human Zoo* reminds us that any species that kills its own kind will become extinct. Implied here is the idea that killing one's own kind is not within the natural order of things; therefore, killing another human being is immoral. Recent studies of certain animals seem to question the "natural law theory" and its claim that goodness exists as a part of the natural order of the universe. Evidence exists in the animal world of gang rape, male rape, and murder of offspring, cannibalism, and territorial wars.

The focus of human rights as being *characteristic of the individual* rests on the fact that one is born a human being. Being human involves the capacity to think, to make free choices, to feel (love, have, joy, sorrow), to recognize oneself as a self, and finally, to make plans (which involves the capacity to think and to anticipate a future).

Several persons have written about rights over the years. The eighteenth-century English philosopher, John Locke certainly has been one of the most influential. His Treatise on Government (1609) had considerable influence on the framers of the American Declaration of Independence. However, two twentieth-century writers have had a considerable impact overall in the area of human rights: Alan Gewirth and Alasdair MacIntyre.

ALAN GEWIRTH (1912-2004)

Alan Gewirth points out a simple but important fact about human beings—a fact recognized by psychologists. Human beings act voluntarily for purposes. *Voluntarily* implies freedom. The basis of all freedom is the making of choices. If you cannot choose, you are not free. Further, Gewirth tells you that human well-being involves having the necessary conditions for performing purposive acts. Conditions such as freedom from physical restraints and the possession of self-esteem are requisites for purposive acts. Performing such acts requires freedom and well-being because they are necessary; you have a right to them.

Gewirth calls freedom and well-being the "generic features" of actions since they characterize all action. Further, the individual must have freedom and well-being in order to act. He also claims that the individual must have whatever further conditions are required fulfilling of needs.

Chief among the necessary conditions is the need not to have others interfering with your freedom and well-being. Second, you, under certain circumstances, have the right to another human being's help. Third, Gewirth states that there is only one ground that every person must accept as the justifying condition for having generic rights, and that is, the individual has purpose her or she wants to fulfill. But are these generic rights moral rights? Gewirth answers the question this way: "To establish that they are also moral and human rights, we must show that each agent [person] must admit that other humans also have these rights. For in this way the agent will be committed to taking favorable account of the purposes or interests of other persons besides himself."[27]

Alan Gewirth's views do not go unchallenged. One of the more prominent Gewirth critics is Alasdair MacIntyre.

ALASDAIR MACINTYRE (1929----)

Alasdair MacIntyre returns to the thinking of the early Greek philosophers and their notion of "good character." In doing so, he criticizes "generic rights" approach to morality advanced by Alan Gewirth. According to Professor MacIntyre, the mere fact that you need something doesn't mean you have a right to it. He claims that "rights" are simply "moral fictions" which claim any objectivity that they do not possess. You cannot derive a right merely from a need. He argues that modern morality must be rejected unless it fits into a larger pattern with virtues as the central point. A case in point: Just because a man needs sex does not give him the right to force himself upon someone else.

MacIntyre does not deny that a given society may decide to establish certain rights for those living within that society. The point being, such rights do not exist prior to or independent of that society. And herein is a problem. MacIntyre states there must be agreement on what the relevant rules are and that such agreement is essential. The very notion of rights is a societal one. He goes on to say that, agreement on what the rules are is necessary for an agreement as to the nature and content of virtue. He states, "this prior agreement in rules is something which our individualist culture is unable to secure." [28] Furthermore, according to MacIntyre, these rules are far from being universal.

Rights then are a social invention, which negates the idea of their being given by God, or that they are a product of Natural Law. What is wrong with that? Different societies have different rights. In one society, it might not be considered wrong to kill newly born females because it is the right of the parent to insure the continuation of the well-being of the family unit. Eskimos used to do this because an overabundance of female offspring might deplete food supplies and negate the economic stability of the family unit. Males hunted and brought food to the family. Females did not.

In ancient cultures, some kings claimed the right to have sexual intercourse with a bride on her wedding night before her husband was allowed to consummate their marriage. The Sumerian myth of "Gilgamesh" points this out as one of the complaints against the kin. In medieval Scotland, the English kings claimed such a right for their troops. The 1995 film, *Brave_Heart* starring Mel Gibson, provides an example of *ius primae noetis* or the "right of the first night." In the Twentieth Century, there was the systematic elimination of Jews by the government of Germany. In more recent times, there has been the ethnic cleansing in Bosnia, the slaughter of albinos in Africa, and purges in North Korea. What is natural about such behavior? In today's world, there are still groups that wish to suppress those with different skin colors, religious views, political views, and different sexual orientations. Is this acceptable in a society that claims to be democratic? Even in America, the "land of the free," black people did not have the right to equal protection under the law until relatively late in the 20th Century. Rights and their equal application are at a crossroads in contemporary America. Witness the struggle over women's rights, student rights, and rights of non-citizens living in the United States, fathers' rights in situations involving abortion, rights of grandparents in terms of their grandchildren, and the rights of children in suing their parents for divorce. All of this leads to the question of diversity. Can a united people tolerate diversity? Do human beings have the right to be different?

The Right to be Different: A Question of Diversity

Lawrence M. Hinman in *Ethics: A Pluralistic Approach to Moral Theory*[29] asks, "If we are seeking to be one, does it mean that diversity should be eliminated?" An equally provocative question raised by Hinman is "What should be the relationship between the one and the many, between unity and diversity?" Both questions go to the heart of a very real modern ethical issue. Does one dare to be different in a free society?

It is now obvious that Americans can no longer ignore the issues of ethnicity and cultural diversity. Hinman points out two reasons why ethicists have ignored these vital areas. The first reason deals with how the individual is viewed. The individual is referred to as an "agent," a dehumanizing term. The client is another term substituted for the human being. It is this idea of the human being stripped of any vestiges of individuality that held sway over most of the early thinking in ethics. Hinman's second reason is that the majority of the studies in moral theory were written by white males, about white males, and for white males. A simple check of the history of ethical development will demonstrate this to be true. Women and minorities are generally ignored. By in large, this has been true until late in the 20th Century. Generally, women and minorities, no matter how well their work had been done, were not given recognition. That is changing; admittedly, it is slow. Certainly one of the outstanding contributions in the area of diversity has been the work of Carol Gilligan.

Gilligan's *In a Different Voice* (1982) became the bestselling paperback book ever published by Harvard University Press Her metaphor of "voices" has brought a powerful and wonderful sensitivity to women's causes as well as those of minorities. Unlike her male predecessors, Gilligan did not ignore the emotional world, the world of individuality. And as with others, she has her critics. Lawrence Hinman is one. He points out that her work is gender-based—as were the earlier works in ethics—that there is a dependency upon descriptive and normative implications. Hinman himself proposes a "Diversity Thesis" in which he sets forth the idea that you are a diverse moral voice and that this diversity is a major source of richness and growth in our moral lives. At some point in time, Jesse Jackson is supposed to have made the following statement about black people: "We came here on different ships, but are now all in one boat." That statement applies equally to all the races on this continent.

Consider these questions: Are you going to use this wide diversity to build strength and greatness or are you going to use it to divide and spoil? Do you have the right to be different? Do you have the courage to be different? For some, the price is too high a price to pay.

The Federal Bureau of Investigation reported 5,922 single-bias hate crime incidents in 2013. Of this 48.5 % were racial. Coming in was sexual orientation hate crimes with 20.8%. These are only figures for reported hate crimes. Add to this the complexities of transgender issues, the increase in the number of paramilitary groups, white supremacy groups and the cocktail of other groups whose agenda appears to be destructive it is difficult to claim the United States is a country in which the rights of all its citizens are respected. Despite the 2015 ruling by the US Supreme Court declaring marriage between gay couples legal, the battle is not yet over. Discrimination itself is not bad; it's when bathed in prejudices that it becomes bad.

The fundamental question: can we, as a nation; tolerate diversity, or must everyone march to the same beat of the drum? What has been your response to hairstyles, male jewelry, and body art? Do nose and tongue rings annoy you? Is inter-racial dating or marriage acceptable to you? All of these are examples of diversity.

Censorship and Violence

One of the major areas in which your rights are being eroded is the right to read, view, and listen to what you want. This includes such literary works as *The Color Purple, Slaughter House Five, Tom Sawyer,* and in recent times, *The_Fifty Shades of Gray.* Included in this list are films, video, photographs, computer communications via email, and such social networks as FaceBook, Twitter, Snapchat, and live performances. The movement to censor what is available for public consumption is not new; the earliest case being the Peter Zenger trial in 1735, which established freedom of the press in the American colonies, and then there is the famous Scopes' Trial in 1925.[30] Any censorship movement is an effort to force a preconceived set of values held by certain persons or groups upon the entire public. School systems, libraries, colleges, and universities and the arts are frequent recipients of censorship attacks.

Society, in general, is held responsible for the inculcation of its values, customs, and mores by the citizenry of that society. The question is not should you nor should you not be allowed to read, view, or listen to whatever you wish. Should young children, for example, watch pornography? Should they be the subject of pornographic films and videos? Should children be subjected to a steady stream of violence and disrespect? One study claims that a person by the time he or she reaches eighteen years old will have viewed 40,000 murders in television programs. Now with phone cameras, the murder scenes are real, body cameras, and dashboard cameras bring live coverage of violence. If you say no to any of these proposed questions, aren't you acting as a censor? Where is the line to be drawn? Is the current rating system used by the motion picture industry and the one advocated for the Music/Video industry censorship? Does the American society really intend what the First Amendment to the

United States' Constitution states—"Congress shall make no law abridging the freedom of speech or press?"

The dilemma crops up in two areas: media violence and pornography. Much has been said and written about the violence in the media with television taking the brunt of the criticism. The nightly news now presents dismembered bodies, pools of blood, cars torn to shreds, people being shot, graphic photos of maimed and starving children. How many times was the now-infamous video of the Rodney King beating by the police shown on television or the killing George Floyd by a police officer? Is there something more powerful about a "live" picture than a "still" photo that is frozen in time?

Research has shown a connection between exposure to violence on television and aggressive behavior by children. Even back in 1995, CBS revealed a study that 19 million children between the ages of ten and fourteen would grow up leading wasted lives; that one fourth were at risk and those killed by violet acts doubled within a year. Jumping forward to 2010, one study found that the most frequent activity of children was watching television and the average child spends 28 hours a week watching television. By the time the average child was eighteen years old, he or she would have witnessed 200,000 acts of violence, including 16,000 murders. Up to 20 acts of violence per hour occur in children's programming. [31]

Research suggests some children are negatively affected by such visualization of violence. Can it be established there is a legitimate need for the preponderance of violence shown on television? Does your right to know include explicit graphic details of a rape? Following is an excerpt from a news article dealing with the rape of a little girl.

A police spokesperson reported that the female child had been fully penetrated by her attacker, the penetration ripping the vagina. Her bloodstained panties found near her mutilated body may contain semen from her attacker. Authorities would not comment on this possibility

Does the public need to know this kind of detail? Is the "right to know" in conflict with the "right to privacy" even if, the victim is dead? Can you think of any justification for the kind of detail given in the excerpt above? Was it necessary for the public to know all the minute details presented in the infamous O.J. Simpson trial?

Here is a case study. Its format has been altered to fit the scenario; however, its concept remains unchanged. The characters have been fictionalized.

CASE STUDY 1.8 (DR. SEYMOUR)

Background Data

Elmwood High School is noted for its outstanding English program. Several of its teachers have received statewide recognition and one was selected as "National Teacher of the Year." The school newspaper, "The Journal" and its yearbook, "The Carolinian" have won nearly every state and national competition in existence. Allan Seymour, actually, Dr. Allan Seymour, is the faculty advisor to both school publications and the winner of the state teacher of the year award.

Dr. Seymour is married, the father of twin teenaged boys, and is a devoted and well-loved teacher. Despite the fact, there are only four black students in his literature class, one of his more popular units of study deals with American black writers.

As was his custom, Dr. Seymour distributed a required reading list to his English classes. This time, he added some of the more recent black writers who had won national and world recognition for their contributions to the field of literature. He spent the first three class periods introducing the works on his reading list. He had been careful to include cross-representation of the genre and had tried to make the list reflect a variation in the level of sophistication of subject matter.

Dr. Seymour assigned small group reports, both oral and written. Students were free to form their own groups. Their reports were to include the biographical background of the authors, summaries of published criticisms of the works, a discussion of the chosen work's central theme, and a conclusion consisting of an appraisal of the work based on the student's perspectives. Guidelines were given to each student to help in the preparation of both the oral and written reports.

The Scenario

During the second week of the unit of study, Dr. Seymour was called to the principal's office where Mr. Barger, the principal informed him that he was to stop using some of the books on his reading list because there had been parental complaints.

Dr. Seymour protested the censorship and insisted that it violated his academic freedom as well as the rights of his students to read. When he asked Mr. Barger if he had read any of the books to which objections had been raised, Mr. Barger admitted he had not. Mr. Barger then told Dr. Seymour that if he insisted on teaching such "junk" in his classes he would bring disciplinary action against him. Mr. Barger refused to reveal who had complained, the number of complaints, the specific books that were included in the complaint(s), or the exact nature of the complaint(s).

Dr. Seymour continued with his unit as planned. The following week he was notified that he had been suspended by the Board of Education for teaching "unfit" material in his classroom. This action was taken without a hearing.

INTERACTIVE FOURTEEN

Directions:

Answer each of these questions.
What is the primary issue in this scenario?
What are the rights involved?
What type of rights are these?
Justify your choices.
What possible conclusion(s) would you suggest for this scenario? Why?
Are the same rights involved in this scenario as were involved in the famous Scopes Case in 1925? You may have to research this on the Internet or pay a visit to your local reference librarian.

Pornography

The plea for censorship of sexually explicit films, videos, and literature is based on the idea that it is bad for you to see and read such things. Not everyone agrees that viewing pornography is harmful or that it results in antisocial or sexually aggressive behavior. In the last century (1969), the United States Supreme Court ruled in *Stanley v. Georgia* that people could view whatever they wanted in the privacy of their homes. In response, the United States Congress funded the President's Commission on Obscenity and Pornography, set up by President Lyndon B. Johnson to study pornography. The Commission found there was no link between exposure to aggressive or erotic materials and the commission of crimes, especially crimes of sex. The President and members of Congress rejected the study. Another blue-ribbon committee called The Meese Commission on Pornography[32], which concluded there was such a link between pornography and sexual crimes. The California Coalition Against Sexual Assault posted two articles (both published at the end of 2009) that have opposite conclusions about the influence of pornography on sexual assault. The first article by Ferguson and Hartley appeared in the journal *Aggression and Violent Behavior* and argues, "it is time to discard the hypothesis that pornography ***contributes to increased sexual assault behavior.***" Michael Flood in the journal *Child Abuse Review* arrives at a different conclusion: "especially among boys and young men who are frequent consumers of pornography, including more violent materials, consumption intensifies attitudes supportive of sexual coercion and increases their likelihood of perpetrating assault."

Over the years two points of view have emerged: First, viewing erotica is bad and should not be allowed; second, and considerably more liberal, viewing erotica is potentially educational and/or entertaining."

Since the 1957 Supreme Court case Roth v. U.S, material may be censored if it is judged obscene. According to this famous decision, material was obscene if it met these three criteria:

It must be offensive to contemporary community standards,

The dominant theme of the work must appeal to the prurient interests in sex, and

The work must be devoid of serious literary, artistic, political, or scientific value.

Unfortunately, this decision did little to clarify the issue because three of the criteria can be operationally different; that is, different communities may hold different interpretations and apply them differently. How do you determine the standards of a community? In another case, Georgia v. the Paris Adult Theatres I and II added more fuel to the already hot fire.

The Paris Adult Theatres were charged with showing obscene films (*It Comes Out in the End* and *Magic Mirror*). After considerable legal maneuvering at the lower court levels, the case went before the United States Supreme Court. It ruled in favor of the state of Georgia's claim that the films were obscene. The decision, a close 5 to 4 vote had Chief Justice Warren Burger writing the majority decision and Justice William Brennan writing the minority report. Chief Justice Burger argued that the state was justified in restricting consenting adults access to obscene material in order to maintain public safety and decent society, including the proper tone of commerce.

On the other hand, Justice Brennan maintained that this decision would inevitably lead to the erosion of free speech.

Again, there was not much in the way of defining what is meant by obscene material or by pornography. For the purpose of examination, the issue may be divided into two basic fundamental questions: Should laws be restricting the consenting adult's access to pornography, and is there anything morally objectionable about pornographic material?

As is so often the case in philosophy and ethics, the definition of terms becomes important. And it is no different in relation to those two questions about pornography. The First Amendment of the Constitution guarantees you freedom of expression.

Beware! Even though this Amendment requires that Congress pass **no law** abridging your freedom of speech or press, the courts have held otherwise. You may not libel, meaning you cannot employing false publication in writing, printing, typing (computers now), signs or pictures maliciously damage another person's reputation. As previously mentioned you may not yell "fire" in a crowded public gathering if there isn't one. Furthermore, you are not guaranteed the right to engage in the commercial distribution of obscene material, pornographic, or both. The definition of terms is paramount for understanding.

Pornography may be defined as pictures, writing, or other material that is sexually explicit and sometimes equates sex with power and violence. There is still another aspect of this definition that needs mentioning. The material must demonstrate an intention to cause sexual arousal.

In applying this definition, would you find Picasso's paintings of nude females pornographic? What about Raphael's "Madonna and Child" which shows the child's genital organs, or Michelangelo's paintings in the Sistine Chapel of God with a naked Adam in a frontal position? What about this passage from Ezekiel of the Christian Bible: *Ezek.23.7-10*? Is it pornographic?

7 She gave herself as a prostitute to all the elite of the Assyrians and defiled herself with all the idols of everyone she lusted after.

8 She did not give up the prostitution she began in Egypt, when, during her youth men slept with her, caressed her virgin bosom and poured out their lust upon her.

9 "Therefore I handed her over to her lovers, the Assyrians, for whom she lusted.

10 They stripped her naked, took away her sons and daughters, and killed her with the sword. She became a byword Among women, and punishment was inflicted on her.

Most people would not call it pornographic; whereas many people found the now deceased Mapplethorpe's photographs of nude males in various sex acts obscene and pornographic. People have found such literary works as *Ulysses* by James Joyce and D.H. Lawrence's *Lady Chatterley's*

Lover as obscene. What has been the distinction? Picasso, Raphael, Michelangelo, and Joyce's works are not considered obscene or pornographic because of the artists' "artistic intent." The Christian Bible's "Ezekiel" is intended to teach a moral lesson. The intent, then, becomes a key in determining the status of material as obscene or pornographic. The *intent* must be to make artistic or teaching commentary. This is certainly different from the arousal of sexual desires. Artistic values, intentions, and effects on viewers or readers become requisites for judging something as obscene or pornographic. Is Raphael's "Madonna of the Goldfinch" obscene because it shows a frontal view of a male child?

Obscene presents a somewhat different problem. Obscene means offensive to accepted standards of decency or modesty; inciting lustful feelings; lewd. The hullabaloo in 2009 over celebrity Roseanne singing the National Anthem while she grabbed her crotch in typical baseball player fashion illustrates the depth of the problem in determining, that which is obscene. Some Americans thought her actions were obscene while others thought they were in keeping with her comedic character. Which interpretation is correct? And that question brings us back to an earlier question: How do you determine the standards of a community? Are passages in the Christian Bible to be considered obscene because they are offensive to the accepted standards of decency or modesty of some people? Who decides?

The arguments for and against the right to view pornography range far and wide. There are arguments, which receive greater acclaim than others do. Those will be considered here. First, consider those arguments that are against pornography.

All pornography demeans human life,

Pornography separates sexual passions from real and genuine affection and love,

Pornography degrades sexual expression and is primarily anti-female,

Pornography destroys religious and moral beliefs about human sexual relationships, and

Pornography leads to violence and other criminal activities.

Those who claim pornography demeans human life state it shows a lack of regard for human dignity. This, the critics say, reduces the human being raw animalistic behaviors. Thus, pornography dehumanizes individuals by reducing them to mere performing automatons.

The second criticism claims the depiction of sexual acts pornographically leaves out the element of love. Sexual passion should be an enhancement of love and is associated with the most intimately profound human experience. In pornography, sex is not related to love.

The third criticism is that pornography degrades human beings. Generally, this charge includes only women because it is presumed to be anti-female. Is it not also degrading to the male?

Women, according to the opposition, are portrayed, as object's physically owned by the male, something to be possessed and then dismissed. A primarily male-dominated scenario reinforces a caveman mentality when it comes to male-female sexual encounters. Further, pornography gives the impression that every man must perform Herculean sexual feats. (In Greek mythology, it is said Hercules married fifty women at one time and impregnated all of them on their wedding night.)

The fourth argument maintains pornography destroys the moral religious beliefs about human sexual relationships. Traditionally, sex is reserved for marriage, sanctioned by the dominating religions of Western culture. It is pleasurable, but its main function is procreation. Pornography denies this and overly emphasizes the pleasure aspect of sex.

The fifth argument is one that has long been used. It claims that pornography leads to violence and other crimes, especially against women. Milton Diamond, director of the Pacific Center for Sex and Society at the University of Hawaii at Manoa states, "There's absolutely no evidence that pornography does anything negative." He further states, "It's a moral issue, not a factual issue." [33]However, the increase in "Kiddie-porn" and its violence has generated concern.

Three arguments for pornographic materials have consistently maintained a degree of popularity.

Pornography can be beneficial,

Sexually explicit material is morally neutral, and

In a free society, you have the right to read and view what you wish.

Those that believe pornography can be beneficial argue that it has educational value when it comes to human sexuality. Further, these advocates claim that useful information is provided, that it benefits those who can't find sexual fulfillment through normal means, and those who participate in the production of pornographic films and videos feel they are contributing to society in terms of its entertainment value.

The second argument in favor of pornography advances the notion that it is morally inert. This means that the sexual acts portrayed are morally neutral. They continue by claiming that as persons are not forced to participate in porno productions, or are forced to watch them, there is no moral violation. Furthermore, pornography becomes questionable only in terms of the morality brought to it by its viewers. The words porno and pornography are viewed as "dirty" words and conjure up all sorts of preconceived notions that may not necessarily be accurate.

The third argument, covered under the First Amendment, is probably the strongest argument of the three presented. If sexually explicit material is taboo and made illegal by government statutes, advocates of freedom ask, "Where does censorship end?"

Any sexual behavior supposedly caused by viewing pornography is a natural lead-in for another major concern in human sexual relationships—sexual harassment.

Sexual Harassment

A newspaper article began with "Birds do it, senators do it, even fuzzy little bees do it, that is, they engage in the ancient art of sexual harassment. Stress it on the first syllable or stress it on the next, but harassment is probably as old as the partition of sex cells into sperm and eggs."[34] But, does that make it right?

One of the major rights issues today is that of the individual to be free from sexual harassment. The issue was forcefully brought to national attention and focus by the United States' Senate confirmation hearings on Clarence Thomas' nomination and appointment to the United States Supreme Court. The Tailhook Scandal (1991) and the Packwood Scandal (1993) continued to place the issue before the American public. There have been other high profile celebrity cases brought to the public's attention since then. Yet, with all of the publicity created by such cases just what does sexual harassment include? Does telling an off-colored joke to a person of the opposite sex constitute sexual harassment? Does commenting about particular parts of a person's anatomy even if they are generally of approbation constitute sexual harassment? Is touching someone on the buttocks harassment? If so, coaches should take notice. Is asking a classmate for a date sexual harassment? A high school in Florida declared asking another student for a date during school hours constituted sexual harassment.

The fundamental issue is a violation of another person's right to privacy of his or her person. That which was once intended as good-natured "kidding around" may now be viewed as grounds for a costly lawsuit or legal charges. There is no doubt that there has been sexual harassment in the workplace and that is wrong. But is it necessary to overreact as in the Florida high school? Where do you draw the line? Examine the following case study:

CASE STUDY 1.9 (MAGGIE & JIM)

Background Data

Maggie was one of the cashiers at an Eastern college cafeteria. She has worked for the college for twenty years. Maggie loved to play jokes on the students as well as the faculty. She was known as a great "kidder." Once she even put a fake worm in the college president's salad.

Some people felt she went overboard and resented being the brunt of her sometimes-bawdy jokes.

Jim Stoltz, a respected professor by colleagues and students, had been teaching at the college for fifteen years. He taught literature, looked like the typical English professor, beard, tweed jacket, baggy pants, and scuffed shoes. Even though he was soft-spoken, he could rise to a dramatic rendition of Keats or Byron. He was easily embarrassed by suggestive remarks or behavior.

The Scenario

As was the custom, the college cafeteria was decorated for the upcoming holidays. Students were busy cramming for final exams and faculty was busy grading last-minute papers. Professor Jim Stoltz frequently went to the cafeteria to grade papers. He usually had a cup of tea and a muffin. The cafeteria employees were dressed as reindeer, packages, and elfin hats.

Jim Stoltz was seated at his usual table. Maggie spotted him and decided it was time to do a number on him. She ambled over to his table.

"Hey, professor, how are you?
"Oh, hello, Maggie. Just fine. Thank you."
Maggie moved in closer, leaned into Jim's head. Her large breasts rubbed against his right ear.
"So, what do you hear, doc?" she asked.
Jim tried to move, but Maggie wrapped her arms around him. His face turned red.
"I said, what do you hear, doc?" She pulled his head closer into her breasts.
Then he heard: "Jingle Bells."
"Ain't that something else? A musical braw?" she said laughing loudly.
He could hear her telling the kitchen staff how she had embarrassed him. Their laughter filled the

room as they looked over the counter to where he was sitting.

INTERACTIVE FIFTEEN

Directions:

Answer these questions and in a paragraph justify your answers for each answer you provide.

Do you feel this scenario is an example of sexual harassment? Why? Why not?

Do you feel the sexual harassment thing has gone too far; that is, that it now denies normal human relations at the workplace? Why? Why not?

If you were Professor Jim Stoltz, would you have felt sexually harassed? Why? Why not?

What if the situation was reversed? That is if Jim Stoltz had rubbed a certain part of his anatomy against a female? Would this have been sexual harassment? Why? Why not? Would this be an example of what is called a "double standard?"

***

GLOSSARY OF TERMS

Descriptive Law. . . Describes what actually happens under certain conditions. Scientific laws are descriptive.

Equality . . . Equal before the law and under its application

Justice. . . Conformity to moral rightness in action or attitude; fair treatment

Natural Law . . . A set of prescriptive rules of conduct within a given culture for regulating its own social life

Prescriptive Law . . . Social rules that regulate one's behavior; customs, mores of the culture in which you live

Teleological . . . The goal of each thing is to be or act in accordance with its distinctive characteristics, which are common to all of its kind.

Telos . . . The Greek word for purpose; the root word of teleological

Realm of Entitlement . . . You are authorized; you do not need the consent of another those things which are yours because you exist.

SUGGESTED READINGS

Allgeier, Elizabeth Rice, "Violent Erotica and the Victimization of Women," in Siecus Report, 11, May-June 1983, pp. 5-6. Sex Information and Education Council of the U. S., Inc. New York.

Assister, Alison. *Pornography, Feminism, and the Individual*. Concord, MA. Paul and Company Publishers, 1991.

Baird, Robert M. & Stuart E. Rosenbaum (eds) *Pornography: Private Rights or Public Menace*. Buffalo. Prometheus Books, 1991.\

Bishop, Sharon, & Marjorie Weinzweig (eds) *Philosophy and Women*. Belmont, CA: Wadsworth, 1979.

Brandt, Richard, *Ethical Theory*. Englewood Cliffs: Prentice-Hall. 1959.

Cline, Victor. *Media Violence, Pornography, and Censorship*. Provo, UT: Brigham Young University Press, 1974.

Clor, Henry M. (ed) *Censorship and Freedom*. Chicago: Rand McNally, 1971.

Dworkin, Ronald. *Taking Rights Seriously*. Cambridge: Harvard University Press, 1977.

Jensen, Robert with Debbie Okrina. "Pornography and Sexual Violence." National Resource Center on Domestic Violence. Harrisburg, PA. 2011. VAWnet.org.

Lock, John. *Two Treatises on Government*. New York: New American Library, 1965.

Melden, A. I. *Human Rights*. Belmont, CA. Wadsworth, 1970.

Segal, David. "Does Pornography Hurt Children?" New York Times. March 28, 2014.

Solomon, Robert C. *The Big Question: A Short Introduction to Philosophy, Fourth Edition.* Fort Worth, TX: Harcourt Brace College Publishers, 1994.

Walzer, Michael. Spheres of Justice: A Defense of Pluralism and Equality. New York: Basic Books, 1983.

Williams, Paul. (ed) The International Bill of Human Rights. Glen Ellen, CA: Entwhistle Books, 1981.

CHAPTER SIX
HUMAN SEXUALITY

If there is an area of human behavior that raises ethical questions, it is most certainly that of human sexuality. It has become even more significant in today's world of freewheeling "bang-bang, thank you ma'am society with its rampant STDs. (gonorrhea, syphilis, human papillomavirus, genital herpes, chlamydia, HIV-Aids) History records the Roaring 1880's but those were nothing compared to the 1990s. In 1992, 354,000 un-wed young women between the ages of 15-19 gave birth. It's cool to be sexually active by age twelve. Young people during this decade represented the single largest segment of the world's population, with over a billion between ages 10 to 19. The number of couples of reproductive age increased worldwide by 18 million a year. Earlier you were asked, "where do you draw the line?" The nature of that question applies to the topic of human sexuality. The dominating attitude about sex is that only appropriate public standards be applied; these being consent and caution to avoid disease and unwanted pregnancies. The assumptions and implications here are astronomical.

Does a less rigid sexual standard lead to unwanted consequences? Looking back at the 1960s, "sexual revolution" we can readily see some of those assumptions and implications. In 1960, 5.3% of all births in the United States were illegitimate; in 1990, it was 28%. Jumping forward to 2012, the data indicated a 40.7 percent of all births in the United States were out-of-wedlock. In 2017 it has been reported that two-fifths of all childbirths were to unmarried women.

What happens when moral behavior is questioned? Don't assume it is the person's sexual behavior that is being questioned It most likely is not; especially with 58% of the population no longer viewing out-of-wedlock births negatively. The implication is there has been a significant shift in "traditional sexual morality." Also, bear in mind that the old adage "what one says and what one practice may be two different things." Are there certain sexual behaviors that are in themselves out and out wrong? Rape may come to mind. What about incest? As noted in the previous chapter, sexual violence against another is wrong and illegal. Certainly, there are sexual behaviors that cause harm in less violent ways than rape. Deception and emotional hurt are harmful frequent by-products of sexual transgression and are painful. Harassment because of gender changes or deviation in sexual organs falls within this area.

In the Judeo-Christian dominated Western culture, certain kinds of sex acts are condemned regardless of any relationship to morality. Generally, these prohibitions involve fornication and perversity. As with other ethical terms, definitions are in order. *Fornication* is sexual intercourse outside of marriage and *perversity* is sexual intercourse, which is not of the kind that leads to reproduction. Bestiality is included as being perverse. Traditional, homosexual intercourse, oral intercourse, anal intercourse, and masturbation are all considered perverse. It appears that the issue of condemnation is "reproduction." Birth control methods that rely upon condoms, intrauterine devices, and or the "pill" fall within the perverse purview. Only "natural" birth control is acceptable and that generally means abstinence.

The complicated issues surrounding human sexuality certainly involve the age-old question dealing with the "good" life. Yet, the statistics on unwed mothers demonstrate forcefully the issue of a lack of moral responsibility. You just don't have a kid and throw it in the "dumpster" of welfare existence. The traditional view of human sexuality may be found in the philosophical considerations of Thomas Aquinas.

AQUINAS AND NATURAL LAW

Aquinas, A Roman Catholic priest, argued that just as there is a proper end or goal for human beings (for Aquinas this was "rational activity."), so too there is an end for each of the separate human faculties or parts. According to St. Thomas, each of your actions should have a proper end. Sexuality by its very nature is directed toward its natural end—reproduction. Human copulation should be open to that natural end. Heterosexual intercourse in which the male sperm is deliberately diverted from its **natural goal** would be perverse. According to Aquinas, fornication is immoral because it fails to respect what is the natural designated law of human sexuality, that is, reproduction.

The Vatican issued a declaration concerning some questions of sexual ethics. It states, in part, "according to contemporary scientific research, the human person is so profoundly affected by sexuality that it must be considered as one of the factors which give to each individual's life the principal traits that distinguish it."[35] The declaration pointed out that the corruption of morals has increased, and of the most serious indicators of that corruption is the unbridled exaltation of sex. The exaltation of sex? Examine the number of magazine advertisements, newspaper ads, radio, and commercials devoted to sensuality. Television makes blatant use of sex appeal in its commercials. Everything from automobiles, baby diapers, and baby-back-ribs, chicken to toothpaste fills the space with sexual innuendo. Television programs are loaded with sex scenes or implied sex scenes. A catalog released by an international book publishing company list over forty titles dealing with the topic of sex. The topics of the books listed included sexual positions, group sex, and how to enjoy self-sex. There is no question about human preoccupation with sex. And its end is not reproduction, as Saint Thomas Aquinas would have it be.

Even though the advocates of natural law view human sexual acts as having intrinsic significance, the procreative act, there are those, who claim procreation is not the only value of sex. The more liberal advocates of the natural law recognize there is a *unitive aspect* to sexual intercourse. By this, they mean sexual intimacy should aim not just at proration but also at expressing and deepening the personal union between the two involved partners. This is not in conflict with the described goal or end of sex—having children. The Natural Law Theorists having children should be within the context of marriage. Because of this belief, the unitive aspect of sexual intercourse belongs within marriage.

You may find the implied advocacy of monogamy interesting. The Natural Law Theorists believe it is this unique aspect of human sexuality that prohibits humans from being reduced to mere baby producing machines. The futuristic concept of going off to a baby-making factory as described in Ayn Rand's novel, Anthem would be unacceptable. In such a case, the human being has been reduced to a robotic status. The massive rapes in Bosnia as a part of ethnic cleansing illustrate a modern idea of reductionism. Those unfortunate women were reduced to a machine status, violated, and impregnated, to produce "half-breeds" (from a religious point of view) that no one would want. The sorrow was doubled because those violated women became undesirable by men of their own faith. Both of these ideas, the rapes, and forced pregnancies to reduce the religious population of Bosnia are an abhorrence to most people. Such aggressive behavior destroys the unitive aspect of sex.

Contraception is one of the areas of human sexuality that commands considerable debate. Those who argue the unitive aspect of human sedulity should take precedence over the procreative aspects view the use of contraception within marriage as justifiable. Others argue procreation is the fundamental good and any unnatural use of contraception (other than abstinence) constitutes a violation of the natural end or goal of sex. The Catholic Church still holds artificial contraception as a violation of the natural process of procreation.

The national and international push to practice safe sex by using condoms is held as inappropriate by many of the natural law theorists. There is an inherent assumption underlying this push for safe sex. That assumption is that you will have sex and since you will, you should practice safe sex by using condoms. The debate will continue because of the unitive aspect of human sexuality. If the unitive aspect of sexuality is indeed primary, then does that include gay marriage? Should these be viewed *as natural*?

As with so many words natural and Natural Law Theory, have several different applications. You may not agree with some of the broader uses of the terms or disagree with them. You do have an obligation to be aware of what they imply.

The natural socialness of human beings as reported by Aristotle and Saint Thomas Aquinas has been replaced by the view that human nature consists of individuals who maintain self-interest rationality. The traditional view emphasized procreation as a fundamental human good, but the more liberal approach, often called the *individualist approach,* emphasizes human rights and consequently leaves no room for a specific sexual morality. Is this the real sexual moral problem faced by contemporary society? Is it true that Americans no longer have a specific sexual morality?

For the individualist, sex is used to further individual self-interest. You are free to act as you choose, as long as you do not violate the rights of others. Sexual partners are viewed as free, consenting individuals. Deception and violence are still held as being wrong because they violate another's rights. Extramarital sex does not pose a problem if both partners agree to it. This is the "open marriage" idea that gained some popularity in the 1970s. For natural rights advocates, marriage is simply another contractual relationship.

Immanuel Kant used natural-arguments identifying procreation as the natural end of sexual acts. This is in keeping with his views that each individual is an "end-in-itself," because in marriage each person has mutually given the whole self to another. Sex outside of marriage, according to Kant, is using your partner as a mere means, and that is immoral.

The ethical theory of **Act Utilitarianism** does not get involved specifically with human sexuality. Essentially, this is because actions are viewed as morally right to the extent that happiness or pleasure is maximized. If sexual actions maximize pleasure or happiness then it is intrinsically good.

This does not imply nor does it mean that those who follow Act Utilitarian Ethics approve of adultery or sexual perversion. They may not view such as unto themselves as wrong, but the unhappiness they may cause is viewed as morally wrong.

Rule Utilitarians are somewhat more specific in that they claim that society determines whether there is a specific utilitarian rule for sexual conduct and that such a rule or rules will have a high degree of acceptance; that they will result in greater happiness than would some other rules. The Rule Utilitarians may not have specific rules concerning human sexuality but they do against violence, deception, and the breaking of promises, and these have an application to human sexual behavior.

Following is a case study based on an actual situation. Names, location, and time have been changed to protect the innocent. The Interactive, which follows the case study, has been modified to allow you to explore some other aspects of moral issues.

CASE STUDY 1.10 (MRS. PETTIT)

Background Data

Mr. and Mrs. Pettit[36] of Los Angeles joined a private club called, *Les Swingers*. Mrs. Pettit, a teacher, and John, her husband, a graphics designer, attended a private party at *Les Swingers*. Present at this particular party was an undercover police officer.

After a couple of drinks, Mrs. Pettit was ready to party.

The Scenario

While her husband was involved in a Trois façons in another room, Mrs. Pettit engaged in oral sex with several men as other partygoers watched. The undercover police officer arrested her. She was charged with oral copulation, which was illegal under the California Penal Code. After plea-bargaining, Mrs. Pettit pleaded guilty to a lesser charge.

After disciplinary proceedings, Mrs. Pettit's teaching credentials were revoked because her conduct involved moral turpitude and as such, demonstrated her unfitness to teach in the public schools of Los Angeles.

Mrs. Pettit petitioned the court to order the State Board of Education to restore her teaching credentials.

The Outcome

The court denied Mrs. Pettit's petition.

INTERACTIVE SIXTEEN

Directions:

Answer each of the following questions.
1. Do you feel Mrs. Pettit's conduct at this private club during a private party was morally wrong? Explain your answer.
2. Do you feel that because others watched her performance makes a difference in the morality of her actions? Why? Why not?
3. Is oral copulation morally wrong unto itself if it is within the realm of consenting adults? Why? Why not?
4. Is there a right to privacy issue involved here or does the fact that Mrs. Pettit performed before a group negates the right to privacy?
5. Using Act Utilitarianism as your theory, justify Mrs. Pettit's behavior. You may not personally agree with her actions. Your response is to be based solely on the Act Utilitarian Philosophy and not reflect your personal feelings or belief system.

The identification of two specific kinds of behaviors involving human sexuality is appropriate.

Those that have an adverse effect on individuals other than those who are the participants and as such should be forbidden by either moral commandment or by law

Those that affect only those participating individuals and therefore should be left up to the morality of those involved.

Do these considerations have an application to the case of Mrs. Pettit? Socially, her acts could be condemned; yet, there is the issue of privacy. Those acts in which she engaged were done at a private club during a private party. The court found her guilty of "outraging public decency." Would there have been public involvement if the undercover police officer had not been present? Would there have been a charge had there been no audience? The State Board of Education of California that found her guilty of moral turpitude. *Turpitude* means baseness or a base act. A base act is defined as that which is devoid of high morals or ethics. You may ask who determines which acts are base and which are examples of high morals or ethics. In this case, society does, that is, the society called the State of California through its legislative powers.

Fundamentally, we have to ask what is the purpose and meaning of human sexuality. Three identifiable positive areas are reproduction, pleasure, expression of love, and liking for others. Even though the traditional purpose of sex, procreation, is listed first, it does not imply that it is the most important nor does it imply the exclusion of others. Two psychologists contend that evolution suggests the purpose of sex is the provision of pleasure. The University of California (at Los Angeles) psychologists, Paul Abramson and Steven Pinkerton[37] maintain that if the pursuit of pleasure is natural and necessary then laws should shift from prohibition to regulation. Such regulation, should, according to these psychologists, focus on health: Prostitutes should demand the use of condoms for the prevention of sexually transmitted diseases. Abramson and Pinkerton argue that sexual activity between consenting adults should be permitted without guilt and that includes gay sex, prostitution, and strip club activity. They do not advocate sex with minors, with unwilling partners or sex that is intrusive on television and the Internet that cannot be electronically blocked.

Accept for the moment the Abramson and Pinkerton notion that sexual pleasure is a natural part of the evolutionary process of human life; does that also imply that birth control is moral? Even though Abramson and Pinkerton contribute much to the literature on human sexuality, they do not include the aspect of love in sexual relationships. Is love part of human evolution? What is love's relationship to pleasure? Not everyone agrees that it is an essential ingredient of sexual relationships.

Annalee Newitz in "Why Do You Want to Get Laid? Mapping Sexual Geographics[38] writes "Thus, while we claim sex is a form of deep human connection, it is—more often, I have found—simply a biological function. Sex is not an accurate way to measure the quality of a human relationship. Like money, it is just a concrete *thing* we used to stand in for actions, which transcend the object world." Perhaps Newitze's most damaging comment may be understood in the following statement: "Associated with intangibles like love and pleasure, sex is not necessarily either of these: it is something you *get* as in the phrase 'I want to get laid.' Often we say 'I want to get laid' in much the same manner as we say 'I want a new jacket.' Both are objects of desire, and both provide material satisfaction. Maybe the song, *Where Has Love Gone* is appropriate after all. What do you think?

Yet, many individuals feel and believe that the deepest and most intimate expression of the love of one human being for another is shown through sexual intercourse. This does not mean that you cannot deeply love another human being without having sex with that individual. After all, human beings, generally, love their children, siblings, parents, and other relatives as well as friends without sexual involvement. Bromance is a good case in point. Sexual involvement with a relative is still considered incestuous and in most states, it is viewed as immoral and illegal. Despite what Freud did to Oedipus, the fact remains that Oedipus did not know the woman who became his wife and property upon his ascension to the throne, was his mother. His final act demonstrates his personal abhorrence.

Another aspect of human sexuality needing to be addressed and one some males may not appreciate, but one that is an essential aspect of morality in human sexuality—freedom, and justice in male-female relationships. Freedom and justice are important concepts to most Americans, nearly as sacred as baseball, ice cream, and apple pie. Both have a strong reaction in contemporary society, especially among males. More will be said about male image later. Some advocate sexual freedom but these same advocates do not always include sexual justice as part of their agenda. For many advocates, sexual freedom simply means being free from sexual restraints. Some groups, for example, NAMBLA, advocate absolute total sexual freedom for men, including small male children. John Stoltenberg in his revolutionary examination of male sexuality, *Refusing to be a Man: Essays on Sex and Justice*[39] claims there is a widespread belief that sexual freedom is an idea whose time has come." He identifies five areas in which the sexual advocates what freedom:

1. Freedom from institutional interference
2. Freedom from legal restraints on sex
3. Freedom from religious and medical ideologies
4. Freedom from outside interventions.
5. Freedom from guilt, shame, and fear.

Stoltenberg ". . . in practical terms [sexual freedom] has meant advocacy of sex that is free from value judgments, sex that is free from responsibility, sex that is free from consequences, sex that is free from ethical distinctions, sex that essential free from any obligation to take into account one's consciousness that the other person is a *person*."[40] One has to ask if Erich Fromm's commentary on love in Western culture—that there is a disintegration of love—has come true.

What does sexual freedom mean? In today's world, it means maintaining a sexual posture that preserves male supremacy over women. To be sexually free, men must dominate and subordinate women. That's just the way it is; always have been, and always will be. Right? Wrong! The caveman with a club in hand, dragging his female catch is a fiction. Unfortunately, its connotative meaning has remained. The social notion of domination and subordination has been eroticized and most likely, this is the singular cause of female abuse. Certainly, *the he-man or the super-stud* is the public male image now personified and glorified in the media, sports, and the motion picture industry.

Have you noticed the emerging new female role in the media—the macho chick? Isn't this a continued example of male domination and subordination of the female? Check the parallels in the clothing that women wear—clothing that is touted as the latest style. Look at women's footwear and the increase in the wearing of "the boot." What about the short hairstyles women are wearing. Are these efforts to neutralize the female?

The chart on the next page showing the characteristics of sexual freedom summarizes what the sexual freedom advocates want. Also, it shows what sexual freedom does not mean, and what personal sexual freedom does mean.[41] The questions for you are worth your consideration: Where do you fit?

CHARACTERISTICS OF SEXUAL FREEDOM

Sexual Freedom Advocacy	Sexual Freedom Does Not Mean	Sexual Freedom Does Mean
Freedom from Restraints	Individuals have Sexual Self Determination	Freedom from Fear
Freedom from Institutional Interference	Individuals Experience the Integrity of Their Own Bodies	Freedom from Guilt
Freedom from Legal Constraints	Individuals act out Their own Integrity within Their Rights to Choose	Freedom from Shame
Freedom from Religious and Medical Ideologies	Individuals have Absolute Sovereignty over Their Own Being	Freedom from Value Judgments
Freedom from Outside Intervention	Sexual Justice Between Men and Women	Freedom from Responsibility and Consequences

With the advent of the modern women's movement in the 1970s and the redefinition of women's roles as well as what women are—a historic shift from the former paradigm of self-sacrifice—there has been a damaging attack upon maleness and all that it stands for. The attack on male behavior has dominated social dialogue. Any male who defends this masculine behavior is accused of sexism; any male who supports fatherhood is accused of debasing single mothers, and certainly, any man who supports his wife's decision to stay at home to be a "home-maker" [whatever that may imply] is accused of limiting her career ambitions and of not allowing her to be all she can be.

The *men's movement* with its "million man march" and its "promise keepers" has been a parade of men hugging one another and openly weeping just because they bonded as males is a strong example of the emasculation of men. Warren Farrell has stated, "Blacks were forced, via slavery, into society's most hazardous jobs; men are forced, via socialization, into society's most hazardous jobs . . . we have long acknowledged slavery of blacks. We have yet to acknowledge the slavery of males." Is androgyny the goal? Should it be? Some women have questioned what has happened to the male mystique, the male image, the role model of values, virtue, authority, protector of all that is worth and good?

David Thomas in *Not Guilty-In Defense of the Modern_Man* (Weidenfeld and Nicolson, 1993) offered a challenge that holds true for the current male image—that of a child molester, of the rapist, of spousal abuse. To support his claim, Thomas points out that the group most at risk for homicide in the United Kingdom, for example, is that of children under the age of one. Who murdered them? Their mothers! Americans have been witness to "infanticide" by mothers in recent years. Is this a moral issue? Is it a moral dilemma? Or is it all created by media hype? What role did a corrupted view of manly behavior play in the Orlando massacre?

What has happened to the idea of sexual justice between men and women? The Stanford University sex scandal involving an outstanding athlete and rapes at other colleges and universities seems to demonstrate there is none. It is apparent there is a lack in current culture— a lack of moral understanding, of understanding moral theory, or a lack of understanding moral decision-making.

GLOSSARY OF TERMS

Fornication . . . Sexual intercourse outside of marriage

Individualist Approach . . . The liberal approach to human sexuality that advocates the unitive aspect of sexual intercourse.

Natural Goal . . . In terms of human sexuality, the traditional view, that the goal of sexual intercourse is conception.

Perversity . . . Sexual intercourse of the kind that doesn't lead to reproduction.

Turpitude . . . Baseness; a base act; devoid of high morals or ethics.

Unitive Aspect . . . Sexual intimacy aimed at deepening the personal union between two individuals.

SUGGESTED READINGS

Angier, Natalie. **Woman: An Intimate Geography**. Boston. Mariner Books, 2014.

Bordo, Susan. **The Male Body**. New York. Farrar, Straus, and Giroux. 2000

CDC Study: "Not Doing It: Fewer high school kids are having sex." Reported: New York Times. June 9, 2016. http:www.cdc.gov/Healthy Youth/yrbs/index.htm.

Chapple, Ron. "The Feminization of America is Bad for the World." Corner Blogs Magazine. Nov. 3, 2015.

Deitcher, David, ed. *The Question of Equality*. New York: Scribner, 1995.

Dynes, Wayne R. Homosexuality: Discrimination, Criminology, and Law. New York: Garland, 1992.

Dynes, Wayne R. **Homosexuality and Religion and Philosophy**. New York: Garland, 1992.

Fairstein, Linda A. *Sexual Violence*. New York: Berkeley Books, 1995.

Foot, Philippa. **Virtues and Vices and Other Essays in Moral Philosophy**. Berkeley: University of California Press, 1978.

Goetsch, David L. "Neutering the Male of the Species: The Feminization of American Society." The Patriot. July 14, 2014.

Lewis, C. S. **Mere Christianity**. New York: The MacMillan Company, 1960, Chapter Five, "Sexual Morality," pp. 74-80.

Serrano, Julia. Whipping Girl: A Transsexual Woman On Sexism and the Scapegoating of Femininity. Berkeley, 2007.

Smith, Jeremy Adam. The Daddy Shift: How Stay-at-Home Dads, Breadwinning Moms, and Shared Parenting are Transforming America. Boston. Beacon Press, 2009.

CHAPTER SEVEN
EUTHANASIA, CAPITAL PUNISHMENT & WELFARE

Euthanasia

Taking another human being's life when he or she has not been found guilty and convicted of a heinous crime generally has been abhorrent to most Americans. There is another approach to taking human life not based on criminal actions— *Euthanasia.*

Euthanasia means the act or practice of ending the life of an individual who is terminally ill or who suffers an incurable condition. The word comes to us from the Greek *euthantos* meaning a good death. Euthanasia involves giving a lethal injection or suspending all life-sustaining treatment.

National interest was focused on the issue of Euthanasia by the Karen Ann Quinlan case. Quinlan, a young woman, had been described as being in a "chronic, persistent, vegetative state." That was in 1975. She remained comatose until June 11, 1985, when she died. Karen's father, acting as her legal guardian, had petitioned the courts to allow the life-support system to be shut down.

Dr. John Kevorkian, a pathologist, created a maelstrom by assisting people in ending their lives. Dubbed "Dr. Death" by the media, Kevorkian who admitted to helping at least 130 people commit suicide was eventually charged with murder. In 1999, he was convicted of second-degree murder in the euthanasia death of a man who suffered Lou Gehrig's disease. He was sentenced to ten to twenty-five years in prison. He served eight years, leaving prison still believing people have a right to die. He died at the age of 83 in 2011.

The issue of assisted suicide was brought before the voters in Oregon in 1994. The voters approved the law and it became effective in December of that year which made Oregon the only place in the world where it was legal for doctors to help their patients die. This legislation caused an ebb tide of concern from the Pacific shores of the United States to the Vatican at Rome. Litigation prevented the law from going into effect. In 2006, the U. S. Supreme Court in a decision 6 to 3 upheld the Oregon Death with Dignity Act.

Brittany Maynard, a 29-year-old Oregonian, ended her life. She became the public image of those who decided to end their lives rather than continue to suffer during whatever time they had left to live. This was in 2014.

The fundamental issue revolves around the question of whether or not people have the right to die of their own choosing or by the choice of their designated representative . . . if they are terminally ill. However, this places the idea of euthanasia into two different issues simultaneously. The issue of the morality of euthanasia itself; the second involves the morality of laws that would make euthanasia legal. Resulting from this double-edged issue are several sub-concepts that come into play: What is a "good death?" What does death mean? What is the difference between "ordinary" and "extraordinary" treatment? Is there a distinction between killing and allowing to die? Is there a difference between voluntary and non-voluntary euthanasia? Is withholding treatment murder? Is there a difference between "mercy death" and "mercy killing? Finally, as illustrated by the struggle in Oregon, whose decision is it anyway; the state's the medical profession, the individual, a caregiver, or designee.

These questions and myriads of others need exploration if the issue of euthanasia is to be approached with any degree of sanity. It is not merely an academic issue. People's feelings, emotions, and belief systems are at play. Their religious and moral convictions suddenly may conflict. That conflict may be internally personal as well as societal.

Generally, euthanasia is associated with the elderly and infirm. However, what about newly born infants that will die if extraordinary measures are not taken? What about lung, heart, and kidney transplants? What about those born only with a brain stem? Should these be allowed to die or should they be given a lethal injection to end the potential years of poor health and surgeries? What about those babies that are born conjoined? If they are separated, one may die. Which one is to live and which is not? Is this mercy killing? Is the effort really to save the child's life or is there parental ego at work in such situations and decisions? Should millions of dollars continue to be spent on these children? Shouldn't they be terminated when keeping them alive is so costly? Is age a factor in deciding who should continue to live and who should not? Is the determining factor based on the type of disease, one's color, or financial standing?

To establish any kind of foundation for dealing with these complex issues it is necessary to understand some of the terms that are used. The word euthanasia has been defined. Yet, it has been confused with such terms as "mercy killing," "mercy death," and "allowing someone to die." There are significant distinctions among these terms, which unfortunately are frequently used as synonyms.

Mercy killing in most countries is legally a form of murder. It refers to killing someone by taking a direct action that would terminate his or her life without that person's consent or permission. This has been noteworthy in the past few years as mates of terminally ill have killed them to stop "their suffering."

Mercy death, on the other hand, means assisting the person to terminate his or her life. It is often called "assisted suicide." The terminally ill and suffering individual asks someone to help end his or her life. Mercy killing and mercy death are not legal in any of the fifty states. Oregon law has been presented previously. It should be noted that the law there would leave it up to the doctors to decide whether to comply with someone's request to be allowed to die. Such requests must be in writing, and the patient must be judged to have less than six months to live. The Oregon law as it was written exempted doctors from civil or criminal liability if they acted in "good faith and compliance" with the law. Who, however, is to determine what is "good faith and compliance?"

Allowing someone to die means there has been an essential acknowledgment that further treatment would have no beneficial effect for the ill person. The ill individual should be allowed to die a natural death. Generally the words "die in comfort, peace, and dignity" are added to the decision making process. This approach does not involve an active involvement in the termination of someone's life. It does involve a decision not to continue efforts to prolong the ill person's life. Could you debate that such a decision-making process is involved in terminating someone's life?

Not everyone agrees with these particular distinctions. Dr. James Rachel, author of *The End of Life: Euthanasia and Morality,* argues there is no morally relevant difference between actively killing someone and passively letting a person die. According to Dr. Rachel, what is important is the motivations or consequences of actively or passively killing someone. [You may find of interest Dr. Rachel's article "Active and Passive Euthanasia" in The New England Journal of Medicine, Vol. 292, 1975, pp. 77-80.]

Several arguments have been advanced for and against each of the three areas of euthanasia. The first to be considered here is ***mercy killing***. Unlike mercy death, it is not done at the request of the terminally ill person. It is a decision made without consultation. Generally, a mercy killing is done on the basis the victim's life is too painful to be continued. Victim is a good word here because the ill person has had his or her freedom of choice denied. Jacques P. Thiroux, author of Ethics: Theory and Practice, disagrees with this. He presents the notion that the ill persons involved are "not fully alive as human beings; rather, they are merely existing as organisms—a network of organs and cells." Thus, to end their suffering is an act of kindness. David Asch of the Center for Bioethics at the University of Pennsylvania released a study in 1996 that indicated that one in five ICU nurses helped a patient die without explicit permission from the patient, doctors, or family members.

A second argument supporting mercy killing, and is equally applicable to the other two areas of euthanasia, is that the continuation of the ill person's life will constitute a financial burden beyond which there is no recovery. Families, as the argument goes, would be reduced to bankruptcy and ruin. Don't forget the emotional drain on family members. It gets old very quickly if you have to go to the hospital once or twice a day every day, day in and day out. After all, family members of an ill person have a right to be free from suffering, also; don't they?

The arguments against mercy killing revolve around two major points: the ill person has had no voice in the decision-making process, and then, there is always the possibility of a cure being found before the ill person expires. The first point raises the question of legal safeguards. Who, for example, who has decided the ill person is suffering and is terminal? Has medical science provided all assistance possible? Or has money had a role to play? If these and other questions are not answered and safeguards are not legally established, can you envision a rash of killings in the name of mercy when in fact they would be outright murders?

What about religious issues? Do any of the five major world religions advocate mercy killing? In Christian teachings, for example, one is admonished not to kill. In Buddhism, one is taught to respect all things. In Hinduism, there is a reverence for all life. Islam forbids mercy killing. Judaism views such an act as an offense against the Author of Life. For those with strong religious convictions, the idea of mercy killing is not something they would consider.

Mercy death is equally opposed on religious grounds—killing is killing whether it is requested or not. Remember, mercy death means a direct action that is taken to end someone's life at his or her request. Probably the strongest argument for mercy death falls within the area of individual freedom and rights. A person, so the argument goes, has a right to do with his or her body as they please. [This is not dissimilar to the argument advanced by the pro-choice advocates in the abortion debate.]

Suppose for the moment that it is conceded that an individual has the right to do as he or she wishes with their body, do they have the right to ask someone else to commit an illegal act? Do they have the right to ask you to end their lives? The reply, though weak, comes in the guise of the idea that human beings put their pets out of their misery when they are suffering, should they do any less for their fellow human beings. Is it necessary to say there is a world of difference between a human being and a pet?

The ***allowing someone to die*** proponents base their arguments on the idea of individual freedom. Simply put, this means that a terminally ill patient has the right to make that decision relating to his or her medical care. If that individual chooses not to have a specified medical treatment, then as the argument states, that individual has the right of choice. "The distinction made here is that a direct action is not taken to prolong the individual's life nor is any action taken to end that life. The individual's illness, whatever its form, is allowed to take its own course.

To accommodate the ill person's desires there are a variety of legal documents available. Among these documents are The Living Patient's Bill of Rights, Living Wills, Directives to Physicians, and Power of Attorney for Health Care. Each state may or may not recognize these documents as legal. Some states have approved legislation that permits a terminally ill person to wear a special identification bracelet, which provides instructions not to resuscitate them if they are found unconscious. This is primarily designed to provide information to emergency medical service personal. However, there are problems with such instructions. The following case study points up one of the potential problems with info-bracelets and the moral dilemma that occurs for EMS personnel.

CASE STUDY 1.11 - MARY AND THE EMS

Background Data

Mary is a fifty-six-year-old woman who has worked hard all of her life, having begun working when she was fifteen. During these working years, she had not been able to accumulate any substantial amount of money. She has enough to get by as long as she stays healthy. Unfortunately, she has suffered two heart attacks and her insurance paid only a portion of her medical bills, especially for her last hospital stay. She has struggled to pay off these expenses and has done so. She cannot afford any more expensive medical bills. Mary lives in a one-room apartment. Her rent and utility bills leave her with barely enough money for basic necessities.

The Scenario

Mary has been feeling rather poorly lately. She realizes she has been putting in too many overtime hours where she works. Alice, a coworker speaks to her.

"Look, Mary, you just gotta slow down. You know you don't look so good. You feeling okay?"

"Nothing but the usual. Just tired. It's been a long day."

"Well, you should take a day off. Do something for yourself. You know, there might be a time when you can't get out and about."

"Yeah, yeah. Alice, you're a good one to talk."

The two women parted, going about their work. Mary had to admit that the chest pains seemed to be intensifying. She had trouble boarding the bus to go home. On the bus, she closed her eyes and tried to breathe slowly. Finally, her stop came. She went into the drug store on the corner near her apartment. There she bought an info-bracelet, the kind that says if a person needs medical attention and found unconscious, there shouldn't be any resuscitation. As far as she was concerned, there was to be no next time. She would live as long as she was supposed to and that was all there was to it. No more hospitalizations.

On Friday morning as she was leaving her one-room apartment, Mary remembered the info-bracelet. She shoved it over her hand and settled it among several other out-let store bracelets she was wearing. That afternoon, just before she was to get off work, Mary's supervisor asked her to work another shift. Mary hesitated for a moment and then agreed. The all too familiar chest pains had been bugging her all morning. She could use the extra money and besides, she thought, I have an hour off before I start the next shift.

In the employee's lounge, she sat down, put her feet up on another chair to rest for a while. Maybe I'll have a cup of coffee before heading back to work, she thought.

Another employee came into the lounge and found Mary on the floor, face down and unconscious. The employee immediately called 911. The EMS vehicle arrived within a few minutes. The paramedics found Mary still had a pulse, albeit very weak. Not noticing the info-bracelet among the others on her arm, the paramedics began immediate resuscitation.

Mary revived and found herself in the hospital. After a two-week stay, she was released. She was told she no longer could work and once again found herself with a pile of bills. Mary sued the EMS and the hospital for not following her wishes as outlined on her info-bracelet.

INTERACTIVE SEVENTEEN

Directions:

Answer each of these questions.
What is the primary moral issue?
What is the primary moral principle?
What are four alternatives?
What ethical theory is involved?
In your opinion, do you feel Mary was justified in suing the EMS and the hospital? Explain your reasons.

***

In Western culture, the arguments **against** allowing some to die are based on a common assumption: human life is to be protected and preserved. The arguments may be summarized by stating that allowing someone to die is the same as refusing them appropriate medical care. It is the job of medical professionals to save lives. Allowing a patient to die is not a medical option for many people in the profession—even if the treatment is painful and causes suffering.

There is a religious argument against allowing someone to die. It rests on the idea that only God creates and takes life. It is His decision; not humankind's.

As medical technology advances and becomes more sophisticated the decisions, unfortunately, will not be any easier. Not only do one's religious beliefs enter the picture but so does one's financial situation, family's emotional stability, and the availability of specialized treatment. Just how far should one go? Should non-human animal parts be used in human beings? Xenotransplantation is not a new phenomenon. It has been around since the 17th Century. It has been unsuccessful until modern times. In 1963, Dr. Keith Reemtsma of Tulane University transplanted chimpanzee kidneys into human beings. Word spread that an organ from a baboon had been transplanted into a human being and cries of foul ethics and outright condemnation by a variety of religious groups played out in the newspapers, radio, and television. One basic question has centered around the breeding of certain types of animals for the sole purpose of providing donor organs to human beings. Do you feel it is an acceptable practice to replace vital diseased human organs with those from an animal raised and slaughtered for that purpose? How different is this from raising cattle for meat products humans consume? Terminal illnesses raise difficult questions and people answer them in different ways. The following case studies illustrate the complexities involved in answering the perplexing question of what to do with the terminally ill.

CASE STUDY 1.12 - (FRED AND LOUISE)

Background Data[42]

Fred and Louise have been married for fifty-one years. Both have been devoted to one another, loving, caring, and trusting. Fred retired and he and Louise bought a condominium in Florida where they hoped to enjoy the "good life." Fred's business ties still made it necessary for him to be away from home several times a year.

The Scenario

Returning from a trip to California, Fred arrived home to find Louise on the living room floor of their condominium. She was sobbing and writhing in pain. Fred called for an ambulance. At the local hospital, a CAT scan revealed severe osteoporosis of the spine. She would end up in a wheelchair.

With the help of a walker, Louise managed to get around. One day while she was out shopping, Fred received a phone call from the local police. Louise had been arrested for shoplifting. Fred could not believe what he heard. Louise had every kind of major credit card with a well-established line of credit on each. Besides, she always carried a couple hundred dollars in cash. Fred went to the police station, settled the issue, and drove Louise home. He simply could not understand her behavior.

Thereafter, Fred paid closer attention to Louise's behavior. He began to notice she had trouble remembering things, where she was going, or what happened the day before. She had trouble remembering what she had had for her evening meal. Finally, Fred took Louise to their family doctor. After a series of tests, it was determined Louise had Alzheimer's disease as well as the crippling osteoporosis.

As the weeks and months wore on, Louise became more and more dependent upon Fred. When it became necessary for him to travel, Louise would throw a temper tantrum. She became afraid of being left alone. If she dozed in her chair and Fred had gone out, she would scream, go from neighbor to neighbor demanding they find her husband. Often when she napped, she would wake up not knowing where she was.

Gradually, Louise could do less and less for herself. Fred bathed her, fixed her hair, and even brushed her teeth. Louise's weight dropped to eighty pounds and she continued to fall and fracture her bones. Fred felt he had no choice but to hospitalize her. There, Louise became violent, ripped out an I-V, and continued to scream. Fred took her back home.

Once back at their condominium, both she and Fred cried. Between their tears, Louise said, "Fred, God, how I want to die. Even though I love you dearly, I still want to die. I can't stand this anymore."

It was her last time of being lucid. She wheeled herself over to their balcony window and stared out, seeing nothing.

Fred went to his study, got his pistol, and loaded it with one bullet. He went back into the living room, walked up to Louise, put the gun to her head, and pulled the trigger. Her body twitched. He felt her pulse. She was still alive. He loaded the gun once more and pulled the trigger. She was still now.

He picked up the phone and dialed 911.

Actual Outcome

Fred was charged with murder, tried, and found guilty. He was sentenced to twenty-five years in prison. At the time of his sentencing, he was seventy-six years old. He is now deceased.

INTERACTIVE EIGHTEEN

Directions

Answer each of the following questions.
1. What is the primary moral issue?
2. What is the primary moral principle?
3. What are four alternatives Fred could have considered?
4. What is YOUR preferred alternative? Why?
5.hat is the primary ethical theory that best fits this scenario? Justify your answer.
6. Do you think Fred should have been found guilty of murder? Why? Why not?
7. Do you think Fred's sentence was too severe under the circumstances? Why? Why not?
8. Identify your own moral system that came into play as you answered questions six and seven.

CASE STUDY 1.13 (ALBERTO)

Background Data[43]

José was a little over a year old, a delightful child and as the saying goes, "the apple of his father's eye." One day he swallowed a balloon his mother had given him to play with. It had become partially deflated. Juliana, his mother, found him unconscious. Not waiting to call 911, she rushed him to the local hospital herself.

The Scenario

Even though the doctors at the hospital described José's coma as irreversible and his recovery was impossible, they did not declare him technically brain dead.

Alberto, the boy's twenty-five-year-old father, was extremely distraught over his son's condition. Because Alberto had just begun a new job, his medical insurance had not kicked in. There simply was not enough money to pay for an extended hospitalization.

Under the laws of the state, life support systems may be removed from patients who show no brain activity. José still showed a small amount of such activity and for that reason, the doctors had not declared him medically dead. The hospital administrators asked Alberto and Julian to obtain a court order to allow them to turn off the respirator.

Because they had been told their only child was going to die and because they had no money to pay legal fees, the young couple waited, not knowing what to do.

On a Sunday afternoon, Alberto went to the hospital to see his son. Sitting on the edge of the bed, Alberto picked up his son, cradled him in his arms, and gently rocked him back and forth. A nurse came in and wanted to know what he was doing.

Alberto pulled a gun, told her to leave the room. He then pulled the plug on the respirator. Holding the returning nurse and other staff at bay with his gun, Alberto continued to hold his son until he was dead. He then gave the gun to the nurse and policeman who had been summoned. Alberto collapsed, sobbing.

Alberto was arrested and charged with murder.

INTERACTIVE NINETEEN

Directions

On a sheet of paper, answer each of the following questions.

What is the primary moral issue?

What is the primary moral principle?

What are four alternatives Alberto could have considered?

Which one of these alternatives do you prefer Alberto to follow? Explain your reason(s) for your choice.

What ethical theory best fits this case? Justify your choice.

What do you think should be done to Alberto? To Juliana? Why?

In making your decision as to what should be done to Alberto and Julian what ethical system did you rely upon? Why?

Perhaps a final question on euthanasia in whatever form it takes is in order: "Is it conscious will or yuppifcation of death?"[44]

Capital Punishment

Crime and the punishment of those who commit crimes involve issues of morality—the issue of social justice. An overview of societal thinking during the past four decades will help set the stage for the consideration of capital punishment in society.

Following the British abolishment of the death penalty in 1965, Americans began questioning the wisdom of executing criminals. In 1972, the United States Supreme Court struck down the death penalty provisions of Georgia state laws. The implication being that similar laws in other states were equally unconstitutional. However, in that same year, the Court refused to declare all use of the death penalty unconstitutional, leaving it up to the individual states to determine their use of the death penalty.

As the crime rate in the United States continued to soar throughout the 1970's people's views about punishment and imprisonment began to change. Back during the 1960s, the dominant idea was rehabilitation. Social critics claimed that criminals were suffering from psychological problems and that psychological therapy was the best way to deal with them—to get them back into mainstream society as productive and worthwhile individuals. One time a man opened fire on people riding on a Long Island train. His attorney's argument proposed the suffered from "Black Rage." In 2013, there was the now-infamous "Affluenza" defense for a young man who, while driving intoxicated, was responsible for the death of others. The opponents of capital punishment have demanded evidence that would prove that the execution of someone for committing a crime prevents others from doing so. They have been quick to point out that imprisonment does not deter criminals; they continue to claim that many of those imprisoned have become "hardened criminals."

As with many social issues, the pendulum has swung back and forth from the fixed punishment of crimes and the reinstatement of the death penalty to the reinstitution of the chain gangs. [In 1994, the United States Congress passed legislation increasing the number of crimes punishable by death. The President signed the bill into law. Texas, for example, since 1976, has executed 537 people. As of mid-2016, they still had 263 people on Death Row. The year 2016 also registered 19 states and the District of Columbia as not having the death penalty.

The issue involves two fundamental questions: Does society have the right to take a human life? Second, does an individual have the right to be free from harm? Those involved in the debate have missed an important aspect of the issue; **what is punishment supposed to accomplish?** This question brings into consideration ethical principles involving punishment. Several issues are involved and these may be formulated as questions.

What is the definition of punishment?

How is punishment different from compulsory treatment?

What acts should be punishable?

Who should be punished?

Who should execute the punishment?

Defining punishment generally involves two viewpoints: retribution and deterrence. *Retribution* implies payment in accordance with the wrong that had been committed. *Deterrence* implies prevention of further wrongdoing. Retribution may include capital punishment. *Capital punishment* is the execution of someone types of crimes he or she has committed. In the United States, capital punishment is invoked for murder (premeditated murder), kidnaping in which harm has been done to the victim or if the victim has been killed or died as a result of the kidnapping, and certain treasonable acts which endanger the citizens of the country.

These two views, retribution, and deterrence are explicit in Kantian ethics as well as utilitarian ethics. Both of these will be brought into focus in the following discussion. First, however, there is another view that holds some interest here and this is the view held by St. Thomas Aquinas.

ST. THOMAS AQUINAS (1225-1274)

Aquinas was a Roman Catholic theologian and philosopher. His *Summa Theologia* (1263-1273) was an effort to systematize all human knowledge by reconciling Aristotle with Christianity. He claimed the real existence of Universals. He includes both retribution and deterrence in his theory of *natural law*. The basic principles of Aquinas' theory prescribe that human beings live in societies and avoid conduct detrimental to the good of those societies. **Justice**, according to Aquinas, is giving each person his due.[45] In short, good things are due to those who act rightly and bad things to those who act wrongly. Aquinas also believes that one's habits are developed by doing and, as such, punishment can enable wrongdoers to become habituated by acting rightly. Punishment aims to deter people from doing wrong to others. In rendering punishment, society deprives the wrongdoer of his natural rights. Perhaps this is why Americans have "bent-over-backward" to insure criminals of their rights? Some now believe that the rights of criminals prevail, and those of the victims are ignored. The recent political emphasis on crime and punishment, gun control, the building of new prisons, and the increase of the use of the death penalty is reflective of this attitude.

John Locke in *Doctrine of Forfeiture* attempts to resolve the problem of the rights of wrongdoers. He states that in committing a wrong the wrongdoer in effect has declared war on society and thus has forfeited his or her rights.[46] Do you agree? Should those who commit acts against society lose their rights? Can persons who have been imprisoned vote? Do prisoners have the right to medical care? Should prisoners have their desire for a sex change be paid for by the government? These questions are not easy to answer. They do demand serious consideration and thought.

Earlier, it was pointed out that Kant and the Utilitarians held views, which included retribution and deterrence. The Utilitarians maintain that punishment should always have as its aim the wellbeing of society. If punishment will result in good consequences for people then it should be given; if it doesn't, it should not be rendered. The good derived should be the deterrence of further crime, protection of society, or the rehabilitation of the wrongdoer. Immanuel Kant, on the other hand, offers a different perspective by proposing strong retributivism. For Kant, deterrence is not an acceptable justification of punishment because it uses a person as a means to the good of others. Justice and laws of the state, according to Kant, are restricted to the duties for which legislation is possible. Duties that require a particular motive are excluded because legislation can concern only external conduct. The law of justice, therefore, is to "act in such a way that the free use of your will is compatible with the freedom of every one according to universal law."[47] Coercion, used to enforce justice, is justifiable because it counteracts its violation. As a consequence, states may enact laws that prescribe coercive punishments. Kant maintains that equality is necessary for rendering any punishment; otherwise, one individual may be treated worse than another may. In other words, Kant supports the notion of having the punishment fit the crime. The major objection to Kantian retributive theory is that it requires punishment even when no good will result (A Utilitarian criticism). Do you think such an approach would cause needless and pointless suffering? Does the execution of a criminal solve the crime problem?

Following is a case study to help you sort out your views about capital punishment.

CASE STUDY 1.14 - (MARY ADAMS)

Background Data

Mary Adams is a single parent with an eleven-year-old son named Tommy. Both are very active in their church and its many functions. Mary sings in the choir, teaches adult Sunday school, and is a member of the Ladies' Auxiliary.

Tommy attends the Christian school operated by their church, lays on the soccer team, sings in the youth choir, and is a member of the Youth for Christ Club.

Both Mary and Tommy attend church twice on Sunday and once on Wednesday evenings.

Alan Plant, a thirty-year-old bachelor, is a teacher at the church-operated school to which Tommy attends. He sponsors the Youth for Christ Club and is active in the young people's activities within the church. He is very popular with parents and students, always helpful to his students, and takes a special interest in their welfare.

The Scenario

Alan Plant is very fond of Tommy, a good-natured boy with dark hair, green eyes, and a radiant smile that greeted everyone he met. Because

Tommy had no father in the household, Alan spent a good deal of time with him. He would pick Tommy up for the soccer games and other church/school activities. Sometimes, Alan would take Tommy to a professional cocker game. There were occasional shopping trips and the once a month camping trips.

Mary began to notice a change in her son's behavior. He no longer wanted to go to church or school. He stopped going to the YCC meetings, missed soccer practice, and grew quieter and secluded at home. When Alan Plant announced a weekend camping trip, Tommy said he didn't feel well and didn't want to do.

Mary and her son had always had a good relationship but it took some prodding to find out what was wrong with Tommy. Crying, he blurted out that Alan Plant was forcing him to participate in oral sex. Mary sickened at her stomach. Then panic set it. Struggling to gain control of her emotions, Mary called the police. Alan Plant was arrested.

As news spread of Alan's arrest, other parents found that their sons had been sexually molested by him. At the trial, on the day Tommy was to testify, Mary arrived early and took a front seat. Tommy would be brought by a person from the Welfare Department. As Alan Plant was brought into the crowded courtroom, he was greeted with jeers. As the judge called for quiet, Mary rose from her seat, pulled a gun from her purse and fired five shots directly at Alan Plant. He slumped to the floor.

The bailiff grabbed Mary, wrestled her to the floor, and handcuffed her. She was immediately arrested and charged with murder. Tommy, screaming, was whisked out of the courtroom.

Tommy was placed in temporary foster care. Mary's defense was temporary insanity.

Actual Outcome

The jury eventually found Mary Adams not guilty by reason of insanity.

INTERACTIVE TWENTY

Directions:

Answer each of the following questions:
Do you feel that justice was served in Mary Adam's case?[48]
Which ethical system(s) come into play in this case?
On what ethical system do you base your answer to the first question?
Is murder ever justifiable? Defend your answer.

The intent has not been to debate the issue of capital punishment, but to explore the ethical issues surrounding its concept. The following two charts summarize the main arguments for and against capital punishment. Arguments for and against capital punishment can be emotional. Often the emotional overtones are based on religious and core beliefs of those involved in the debate. Can you think of arguments in favor of or against capital punishment other than those presented in the two charts? Do you feel building more prisons is an answer to the problem of crime in the United States? What are your feelings about the use of "chain-gangs" as punishment? Do educational programs and rehabilitative programs make a difference in the crime rate in the United States?

Arguments For

    Capital punishment deters the killer from killing again because of his/her execution
    The cost of keeping a person in prison has become prohibitive
    There is no proof that rehabilitation works
    The idea of capital punishment strengthens the entire criminal law system of the country
    A person who murders another forfeits his/her rights
    Capital punishment is simply a form of self defense
    There is a psychological benefit to family members of the victim as well as to society as a whole.

Arguments Against

Drugs and other means used in the exaction process are in humane

It Capital punishment violates the societal idea of human life is of value

Execution of the criminal will not return life to the victim

There is no concrete evidence to support the claim that capital punishment is a deterrent to further criminal acts by others

Inequality in rendering judgments happen all too often

Execution denies any chance of rehabilitation

makes the person(s) doing the execution a murder.

Welfare

Certainly one of the more heated social-ethical issues is welfare. The clamor across the country ranges from "stop paying people to have kids out of wedlock," to "no work; no pay," to "no more food stamps for immigrants." Welfare and its related issues become more volatile during political campaigns. Questions such as what is the government's obligation to its citizens? What rights do individuals have in terms of their well-being? Does one have the right not to go hungry, to have medical attention when it is needed, and to have adequate shelter? Does one have the right to a decent job or does one have to accept work below the average wage? What is the proper role of education in society? Should everyone have free public education? Should colleges and universities be free to all citizens? Should those who have less mental abilities be siphoned off to "training schools?"

Philosophers, psychologists, sociologists, social reformers, politicians, ethicists, religious leaders, and humanitarians in all walks of life have wrestled with these and other related questions for a long time. The bottom line in all of their discourse is this: *All human beings have equal rights to the necessities of life.*

Reasonable and rational thinking quickly demonstrates the intensity of the problem. Can society support its nonproductive members indefinitely without bringing suffering to those who are productive? [Those persons who are in prisons are considered nonproductive, for example.] Does one who is dependent upon society for support have a moral obligation to that society? If so, what is the nature of that obligation?

According to the United States Census Bureau in 2011, over 100 million people received welfare benefits from one or more government programs. That's approximately 35% of the national population. CNS.com reports (2012 latest figures available) the number of welfare recipients surpassed the number of full-time workers in the private sector.

There is little question that the United States has a problem. What is the solution? Now there doesn't seem to be a viable solution. Society still believes that welfare is anti-work and anti-family, but what are the basic issues? Isabel V. Sawmill in Welfare Reform: An Analysis of the Issues lists four areas of criticism.

1. The welfare system hasn't provided sufficient state flexibility

2. The system doesn't encourage work

3. The welfare system is responsible for the breakdown of the family, especially for a rising tide of births to unmarried women,(nearly 44% of the births in the US were to unmarried women 2014) and

4. The system has done little to reduce poverty, especially among children.

Despite these criticisms and others like them, there has been little agreement on what should be done. History of past reform attempts demonstrates credence to these charges. If welfare is such an issue, such a controversy, and such a burden, why bother. Is there a moral obligation here?

W. D. Ross' *prima facie duties* come to mind. His duty of beneficence, helping to improve the conditions for others applies. As a human being, are you not obligated to help prevent suffering? A counter-question: What if helping others causes you to suffer? Are you obligated to suffer? Utilitarianism suggests that it may be necessary for some people to suffer if that suffering produces the greatest good for the greatest number. Should the greatest number, the majority, always have its way just because it is the majority? Likewise, should the majority always yield to the minority? These questions are difficult; answers are even more difficult.

Education of all the people and their children has not brought a solution. Yet, education is continually tied to welfare issues. Does having an education guarantee you a productive life? Does education guarantee that a recipient of welfare will no longer need public assistance? Would the field of psychology have more to offer than "formal instruction" or "job training" for the development of a skilled labor force? Is the current emphasis on job-skills training an answer especially when many of those skills taught are outdated by the time the training-program is over? Advancements in technologies are job killers as well as creators.

What about the victims of downsizing or of the work being sent out of the country who are well educated and trained who suddenly can't find work? Does corporate America have a moral obligation?

All human beings have equal rights to the necessities of life. But doesn't that, unto itself create societal obligation? Equal rights do not mean a free ride. It does imply taking responsibility and therein lays the problem. How do you get people to accept responsibility for their own wellbeing? How do you get people to be accountable? Formal education, as attractive as it may seem, has not provided the answers. Do you think it should? Can it? (For a discussion of the American educational system, see my book, DUH! The American Educational Disaster)

INTERACTIVE TWENTY-ONE

Directions:

Create a scenario in which you deal with one of the following welfare issues:

A woman, unmarried, with five children, is pregnant again.

A man claims he can't work because of a bad back.

A young couple, out of work, living on the streets, wants job training.

An elderly woman, living on a low social security check, needs help to get necessary medicine.

A young man who has lost his job because he has HIV-positive needs living and medical assistance.

In preparing your scenario, assume you are the caseworker at a local welfare office and one of the above has come to you for assistance. You are to create the problem, provide alternatives, and arrive at a preferred outcome. Identify which philosophy you are using.

***

GLOSSARY OF TERMS

Allowing someone to die . . . the withdrawal of medical treatment so that a terminally ill person may die naturally

Capital punishment . . . the execution of someone for committing certain types of crimes

Deterrence . . . prevention of further wrongdoing

Doctrine of Forfeiture . . . proposed by John Lock; states that a person who commits a wrong is in effect declaring war on society and thus has forfeited his or her rights

Euthanasia . . . the active practice of ending the life of a terminally ill person by humane means

Justice . . . giving each person his or her due

Mercy death . . . assisting a terminally ill person in ending his or her life; often called assisted suicide

Mercy killing . . . taking an action to end a terminally ill person's life without that individual's permission

Natural law . . . a theory of St. Thomas Aquinas in which he proposes that human beings live in societies and avoid conduct detrimental to those in that society

Retribution . . . payment in accordance with the wrong that has been committed.

SUGGESTED READINGS

Bayles, Michael D. & Kenneth Henley. ***Right Conduct: Theories and Applications.*** New York: Random House, 1983

Bedau, Hugo & Paul Cassell (eds) ***Debating the Death Penalty.*** New York. Oxford University Press. 2005

Haugen, David. ***The Death Penalty.*** Farmington Hills, MI. Greenhaven Publishing, 2013

Johnson, Ruck C. et.el. Mothers' Work and Children's Lives: Low-Income Families after Welfare Reform. W. E. Upjohn Institute of Employment Research, 2010

Olen, Jeffery & Vincent Barry. ***Applying Ethics: A Text with Readings, Third Edition.*** "Chapter Seven, Capital Punishment." Belmond: Wadsworth Publishing Company, 1989.

Seawall, Isabel, et.el. Welfare Reform and Beyond: The Future of the Safety Net. The Brookings Institution. 2004

CHAPTER EIGHT
ETHICS AND THE ENVIRONMENT

Perhaps you have seen photos of an atomic bomb explosion—unmistakable giant mushroom-shaped cloud billowing ever upward. It has become the punctuation mark for modern civilization. With the advent of this horrific phenomenon, the world changed forever, becoming aware that human actions could negatively affect other human beings as well as the environment in new and heretofore unheard-of ways.

Since that first explosion, many have come to realize that other things can and do have just as serious effects on human life as that first detonation of an atomic bomb. New drugs, foods, chemicals, and technologies, as well as new uses for old ones, may produce deadly effects as well as the touted benefits they claim to offer humankind.

A man is truly ethical only when he obeys the compulsion to help all life, which he is able to assist, and shrinks from injuring anything that lives. He does not ask how far this or that life deserves one's sympathy as being valuable, not—whether and to what degree it is capable of feeling. Life as such is sacred to him. He tears no leaf from a tree, plucks no flower, and takes care to crush no insect.
Albert Schweitzer

Back in 1958, a famous company used the slogan, "progress is our most important product." But what do we mean by progress?

Does destroying an orange grove, a stand of trees, an orchard for a new shopping center, or drilling an oil well in a pristine natural area that produces a harmful environment for sea life, progress. A new age of environmental concerns was born with that kind of question.

Nearly everyone is familiar with the bald eagle, the manatee, and or the spotted owl. They have been on the endangered species list. Have you heard of the furbish louseworts? Like the eagle, manatee, and the spotted owl, they are on the endangered list. They grow in man along the St. John River. It's a rare plant and a member of the snapdragons. A new hydroelectric plant, requiring a dam, was in the works and its creation would kill off this plant. Environmentalists admitted that the plant had little commercial value, that it was not pretty, and had no lovely odor. The dam would provide hydroelectric power, recreational opportunities, and increase real estate values. So what was the big deal? Why was it so important to save a plant? It is on the National endangered species list and it is there because the St. John River area is the only place in the world it is found.

Florida spends millions of dollars to protect an animal that is not eatable, not particularly beautiful, and has no apparent commercial value, the manatee. In Oregon, the issue has been one of jobs in the lumber industry because of the spotted owl.

Admittedly, spotted owls do eat rodents; other than that, of what other value are they. The reintroduction of wolves in certain areas of the west brought controversy. For what purpose? Is the purpose to weed out the deer and elk herds? At the same time, once again, wolves are the object of the hunt. Isn't that counter-productive?

Another area of environmental concern is that of toxic chemicals. Simply put, toxic chemicals are any chemical or gas that creates a harmful effect on the environment. The EPA states (2016) there are 187 toxic air pollutants currently in existence. Among those toxic chemicals are benzene, perchloroethylene, dioxin, methylene, and toluene. Then there are several pollutants in the groundwater: gasoline, road salts, pesticides, and fertilizers. When one realizes that 51% of the population depends on groundwater and of that, 99% of our rural population is groundwater-dependent pollution becomes a major issue.

With the pollution of our air, groundwater, and the soil one has to ask what about the food we consume. Nearly monthly, there is a food recall, and E.coli and or salmonella plague our restaurants. Widespread concern about coal and oil land and sea transport play out a drama as national news broadcasts mining disasters, train derailments, oil spills, and tanker fires. Billions of tons of pollutants puff into the air by uncontrolled manufacturers and by millions of automobiles, trucks, and planes that grace our highways and airways. The rain forests' rape is a world disaster. None of this touches the multiple issues of global warming and climate change.

Two examples, both from the 20h century will point out a fundamental issue that illustrates our need to reign in the untested use of chemicals: DDT and Agent Orange. During the late 1940s and early 1970s, millions of pounds of DDT ended up in the waters off Southern California's coast. What were the costs to ocean life and birdlife? DDT is a pesticide used to spray crops, shrubbery, lawns, and other vegetation. African nations used it to kill malaria caring mosquitoes. Wherein is the fine line of judgment as to what should be sacrificed?

During the Vietnam War, in an effort to eliminate the forest cover of the North Vietnamese and Viet Cong, the United States Military prayed a chemical mixture of defoliants called Agent Orange over 4.5 million acres. Nineteen million gallons of the herbicide filled the air for miles. Dioxin, the chemical used, caused severe side effects.

According to a 2011 report by the Aspin Institute, there is sufficient evidence connecting soft-tissue sarcoma, non-Hodgkin's lymphoma, chronic lymphocytic leukemia, hairy-cell leukemia, Hodgkin's disease, and chloracne. In addition to these dreadful diseases a connection from Agent Orange and Parkinson's disease, porphyria cutanea tarda, ischemic heart disease, hypertension, Type 2 diabetes, peripheral neuropathy, and change of the larynx, lung, bronchia or trachea, and spina bifida in exposed people's offspring.

Now considered harmful to humankind, both DDT and Agent Orange have a major negative health impact on those subjected to them. Do the federal government and the manufacturers of DDT and Agent Orange have a moral obligation to those who suffer from DDT and Agent Orange exposure?

In addition to this question, many more questions need answers. What about the exhaust from the millions of cars, trains, boats, planes, and trucks? Does the consumption of oil, gas, and coal have an environmental cost? Should we continue to rape the rain forests to satisfy the gluttony of greed? Are humans breeding themselves out of existence? Should there be some kind of population control? What about human rights in procreation?

Is experimentation on animals justifiable? Do we have an obligation to consider your relations to other living things in the world? The late Carl Sagan tells us "the earth is experiencing an unprecedented global environmental crisis." [49] That was in 1991. Today we talk about global warming. If what environmentalists say is true, we have not made many significant improvements since Sagan issued his warning. Environmental issues are societal issues.

CASE STUDY 1.15 (U.S. V. MONTROSE CHEMICAL CORPORATION)

Background Data

For 30 years, (1940-1970's) the Montrose Chemical Corporation's manufacturing plant at Torrance, California, dumped millions of pounds of the pesticide, DDT into the ocean. Various species of birds in the ocean off the Southern coast of California suffer elevated levels of DDT. The state of California banned certain contaminated fish from commercial use. Water and shoreline birds along with raptors such as the Bald Eagle still suffer from DDT contamination.

During this period, Montrose claimed DDT was safe.

In 1990, the EES (Environmental Enforcement Section) filed a lawsuit under the Federal Superfund Law. The last claim settled in 2001. Over 140 million dollars paid by the various defendants went into interest-bearing escrow accounts, for the use of the U.S. Environmental Protection Agency, and by the Montrose Settlements Restoration Program.

INTERACTIVE TWENTY-TWO

Directions:

Answer each of the following questions.

Do manufacturers have a moral obligation to do no harm? Why? Why not?

Did the Montrose Chemical Corporation violate any moral or ethical standard? If so, what?

What philosophy applies here? If you feel there is more than one, list all of them.

Do you believe the punishment rendered by the court was fair or unfair? Why?

You might agree that the prevailing attitude and treatment of the natural world is wrong and that human beings need to consider important changes in their laws, practices, behavior, and actions concerning environmental welfare. If not, perhaps you are willing to admit that there are problem areas in the treatment of the environment. Perhaps you feel it is simply a matter of attitude. Yet, not everyone agrees that the problems lie within an ethical disdain. William K. Frankena[50], for example, claims, "What is wrong is not due to our ethics but to our failure to live by them." [Isn't that an ethical issue unto itself?] Frankena provides a quick overview of eight ethical systems with the conclusion that one is more satisfactory as an environmental ethical theory than the others are. The eight theories listed by Frankena are:

Ethical egoism

Humanism (Personalism)
Sentientism
Reverence for life
Everything should be morally considered
Theistic Ethics
Combination Ethics
Naturalistic Ethics

Frankena does not deny that many people do in fact act out of thoughtlessness and self-interests. He believes that all past and present ethical systems embody within themselves an ethics of the environment because they tell what you may or may not do, and what should and should not do about the world around you. He claims the question is not which ethical system, but which is the most satisfactory? Discounting seven of the eight as not being fully adequate, Frankena supports only one.

He proposes the third theory, Sentientism, which includes all sentient beings, as the most satisfactory. Unfortunately, few details are given as to why this approach should be viewed as more satisfactory than the other seven. It seems, therefore, that the question to be asked is which ethical system best provides for all living and non-living things. However, what are the environmental issues to which such an ethical theory must apply?

Even though I raise many questions in the first part of this chapter, the fundamental environmental issues are yet to be specifically identified. The Contemporary Environmental Issues Chart below divides the issues into general categories. They have not been given any priority; nor is the list exhaustive. A more exhaustive list follows the chart.

CONTEMPORARY ENVIRONMENTAL ISSUES CHART

AIR	SOIL	WATER
CFC Emissions	Toxic Dumping	Industrial Run-Off
Industrial Emissions	Over use of Fertilizers	Pesticides & Toxic Dumping
Human EeEE Emissions	Land Use	Depletion

ANIMAL /PLANT	HUMAN
Unrestricted Breeding	Use of Resources
Endangered Species	Population
Use in Experimental laboratories	Diseases

According to Timothy O'Riordan in "Frameworks for Choice: Core Beliefs and the Environment"[51] environmental ideologies are shaped by four basic tensions.

The desire for dominance and reality of dependence

The tension between efficiency and equity

The demands of the present and those of the future

The tension between property rights and responsibilities

Two words focus the nature of these tensions on the impact of environmental issues: technocentrist and ecocentrist. O'Riordan defines the technocentrist as one who is optimistic, managerialist, hierarchist, and reductionist. The ecocentrist, on the other hand, is defined as one who is cautious, accommodating, egalitarian, and holistic. Perhaps the older terms of industrialist and conservationist are no longer appropriate but they still convey the notion of conflict over the management of the environment. Whichever terminology you prefer, there are certain identifying characteristics of these two groups you should keep in mind. The chart below, Characteristics of Environmental Ideologies,[52] summarizes these characteristics.

ECOCENTRIST	TECHNOCENTRIST
Lacks faith in modern technology	Believes economic grown & resources can continue indefinitely
Materialism for own sake is wrong	Accepts new project appraisal techniques & decision review arrangements
Recognizes the importance of the natural world to human beings	Believes human beings can always find a way out of their difficulties through science, technology & politics
Believes endangered species have rights	Harbors suspicions about attempts to widen projects to a large participatory level

Consider the issue of animal rights. A few relevant facts will help demonstrate concern about the issue. Back in 1993, Gillette used over 2,000 animals to test its toiletries. Every year 25 million rats and mice are used in experimental laboratories, of these 85 percent die. Of this 25 million, 500,000 to one million are killed just to test cosmetics. Is it fair to tell you that when you use eye shadow, lipstick, or shaving cream you are responsible for the death of an animal? Not a very nice thought, is it? Yet, should you be blinded because some eye makeup is not safe? And therein lies the rub, who has priority—animals or humans? That was then. What about now? According to PETA, "each year, more than 100 million animals—including mice, rats, frogs, dogs, cats, rabbits, hamsters, guinea pigs, monkeys, fish, and birds—are killed in U.S. laboratories for biology lessons, medical training, curiosity-driven experimentation, and chemical, drug, food, and cosmetics testing."[53]

Americans house over 70 million dogs and over 80 million cats. Unfortunately, many pet owners do not take proper care of their animals. A fertile cat produces three litters of kittens per year. In seven years, one female cat and her offspring will produce 4 20,000 cats. Dogs generally produce only two litters per year and have produced 67,000 births over six years. Shelters and veterinarians euthanize newly ten million cats and dogs every year. Where do you draw the line? Do you have a responsibility for your pets' fertility? Does the irresponsibility of pet owners reflect an attitude of disdain for the environment? Does it reflect Frankena's claim that people fail to live by their ethics?

The dog and cat problem dwarfs next to the issues surrounding clean water and safe foods. Chickens come close to America's love affair with beef especially as it becomes more health-conscious. Over 90% of the chickens and eggs, you eat come from factory *farming*, a billion-dollar business. Factory farms are composed of a series of windowless buildings, each holding as many as 100,000 animals. You may wonder why the concern. A 60,000 bird-egg factory, for example, produces 82 tons of manure every week. Simple multiplication reveals the staggering extent of the problem: what do you do with 4264 tons of chicken manure? When applied to the national level, all "crop-animals" produce two billion tons of manure each year, ten times more than that of the human population. Unfortunately, there aren't sewage disposal systems for the effluent from these animals. Consequently, rain and snow mix with this manure and seeps into the water systems creating a variety of health problems. These animal factories are the biggest contributors to polluted rivers, lakes, and streams than all industrial sources combined. [54]

In June of 1995, this type of environmental hazard was given dramatic impetus when 25 million gallons of hog waste spilled into the New River in North Carolina. The Chesapeake Bay area is highly polluted with nitrates because of the 550 million chickens in the factory farms surrounding the area. New York City's water is polluted because its watersheds are polluted by dairies surround the area. Perhaps the most tragic example of the damage caused by animal effluent occurred in Wisconsin, a state noted for its dairy products. There, cow manure carried a microorganism called cryptosporidium what ended up on the water supply of Milwaukee causing widespread dysentery and even death. This was in 1993. Because of the nitrates, phosphorous and other minerals in manure, streams, rivers, and lakes soon become oxygen deficient and the fish and plant life dies. Yet, you do have to eat, don't you? What is the answer?

Responsible management or respond to consumer demands for more and more. At the end of this section, Case Study 1.16 illustrates one of the four basic tensions outlined by Timothy O'Riordan.

The *Flint water crisis* is a drinking water contamination issue in Flint, Michigan, the United States that started in April 2014. After Flint changed its water source from treated Detroit Water and Sewerage Department water (which was sourced from Lake Huron as well as the Detroit River) to the Flint River (to which officials had failed to apply corrosion inhibitors), its drinking water had a series of problems that culminated with lead contamination, creating a serious public health danger. The corrosive Flint River water caused lead from aging pipes to leach into the water supply, causing extremely elevated levels of the heavy metal. In Flint, between 6,000 and 12,000 children have been exposed to drinking water with high levels of lead and they may experience a range of serious health problems.[55] The United Way estimates it will cost $100 million to help the children contaminated with lead. [56] What is the moral obligation of government officials and employees to the public they serve?

CASE STUDY 1.16 - (JONES VS ATLAS CONSTRUCTION COMPANY)

APPENDIX A

Background Data

Bob Jones is a chicken farmer as were his father and grandfather before him. The family has lived on the same large tract of land for several generations. When a son or daughter married, the spouse moved onto the farm to live, work, and raise a family. That's the way it had been since the early 1800s and that was the way the family intended it to continue.

The farm consisted of several houses, outbuildings, and a variety of sheds. Behind these buildings were neat rows of hen houses, each of the ten buildings each contained 1500 chickens.

Tom Atlas and his construction company's newly planned up-scale housing project, a short distance from Jones' contained a small stream, which originated on the Jones' farm. One day the health department came through to check the water supply for the new project.

Finding the water loaded with nitrates, the health department withheld approval of the project. Tom Atlas was furious. Unless he could get the approval of the health department, his project would be doomed and he would lose millions of dollars and be ruined.

The Scenario

Tom ordered his supervisor to move some equipment and block that stream. The supervisor reminded Tom that blocking the stream would flood out the Jones' farm.

"Don't argue. Just do it. And do it now!" Tom ordered.

Bob Jones heard the bulldozer because it was making short stops and go it caught his attention. He jumped in his jeep and drove down the road a couple of miles. He stopped his jeep and watched the man fill in the creek. He felt the anger creep into his face, slammed the jeep into gear, and drove onto the construction site. He stopped, jumped out of the jeep, and confronted Tom Atlas. They argued.

"Get off my property and stay off," Tom bellowed as Bob spun out in the jeep, spewing dirt in Tom's face.

Once back at the farm, Bob called the sheriff and filed a complaint. He said, "They don't have the right to deny me a living. Tom Atlas has no right to dam up the creek and flood me out."

The sheriff went out to the construction site and spoke with Tom Atlas.

"Look, sheriff, this is my property and I can do with it what I want. Besides them chickens are polluting the land as well as the water. Look at this report from the health department. I'm building fifty homes. Look at the work I'm providing for the locals, the taxes being brought in because of my development. That's more important than a few thousand chickens."

"Hate to do this Tom, but I have to serve you with this warrant. The judge has ordered a cease order."

The sheriff left. Tom went into his office trailer, made a phone call.

The next morning there were a dozen or so people with picket signs protesting the pollution of the local water.

INTERACTIVE TWENTY THREE

Directions:

Part One:

Answer each of the following questions.

1. What type of tension is being illustrated in this scenario?
2. Which person do you tend to favor, Bob Jones or Tom Atlas? Give reasons for your choice.
3. According to the chart, Characteristics of Environmental Ideologies on page 188, which characteristic best explains your point of view in terms of the scenario?
4. Which ethical theory do you think would best apply to this case? Why?
5. What is the primary moral issue?

6. What is the primary moral principle?

Part Two:

Imagine you are an attorney representing either Tom Atlas or Bob Jones, What would your argument be and on what moral philosophy is it based? On a piece of paper, jot down your salient points. Remember, you are arguing from an ethical point of view.

***

Another major problem in many areas is **LUST**, an acronym for "leaking underground storage tanks" They are a source of groundwater pollution. According to the EPA in 2013, there were 563,000 underground tanks in the United States. Many of these contain hazardous waste and fuels. An estimated 5% of these are leaking. Two past issues serve as illustrations for the problems faced with LUST.

During the 1940s the Hooker Chemicals and Plastic Corporation began storing hazardous waste in steel drums and then dumping these drums into an old canal. These drums contained some 22,000 tons of toxic materials. In 1953, Hooker Chemical and Plastics Corporation covered over the site containing the drums and gave the property to Niagara Falls' school district. The old canal called the Love Canal after William Love, its builder, became the site for a school, recreational fields, and nearly 1,000 homes.

Then in the late 1970s, Love Canal residents became aware of odd smells and that their children often had strange burns on their skins. A citizens group began health studies of the area and found a high incidence of several types of physical disorders. Because of the vast amount of publicity received by these informal reports the state of New York began formal studies in 1978 which resulted in the closing of the school and the relocation of some of the residents who lived closet to the old canal. The remaining 700 residents finally convinced the federal government to declare the entire region a disaster. Nearly all of the families relocated and the site closed and capped.

The EPA spent nearly $275 million to clean up the site. Where did the money come from to do this? The taxpayer. In 1990, the EPA announced part of the Love Canal was suitable for inhabitation and was renamed Black Creek Village. However, the Office of Technology Assessment has predicated a "clean-up" will most likely again be declared unsafe. How many infected children this time? How many cancer victims?

Moving forward to 2011 repair work to the sewer released toxic chemicals that residents claim has caused birth defects, cancer, and other diseases. Marlene Kennedy in an article dated February 24, 2014 (Court House News) states more than 500 plaintiffs claim "negligent, reckless, and/or ineffective remediation." The Buffalo News claims there are 1000 plaintiffs. The Love Canal continues to symbolize environmental disaster.

One last example of the lack of concern for our natural world presents a sad story and all in the name of scientific progress. The demise of the Dusky Seaside Sparrow at Merritt Island, near Titusville, Florida is a prime example. You know this area as the Kennedy Space Center. Formerly called Cape Canaveral back in the 1950s, it was the site of the Jupiter-C rockets launched by the United States Army. The Dusky Seaside Sparrow lived and died with a mile or two of Titusville. In 1961, President Kennedy designated this military testing ground as a permanent launching site for the then-new space program. NASA brought an additional 80,000 acres on Merritt Island and began the construction of the space center. At this time there were about 6,000 Dusky Seaside Sparrows, however, by the time of the Apollo, there were less than 2,000. In 1980, a careful search, found only six, all males. In 1986, the only surviving bird lived in an unmarked cage at Walt Disney World's Discovery Island at Orlando. He was called Orange Band, overweight at one ounce, blind in one eye, gout ridden and unsteady on take-offs and landings. With his death, came the end of an entire species. Johnathan Weiner summarizes the disdain for environmental ethics so eloquently that it deserves a space here.

We talk about a space race. There is a space race down here on the ground. In this race, every human being is a superpower and the competition no longer stands a chance. Other species are bound to this or that patch of turf, and this to this planet. We feel bound to no patch of turf on Earth, bound only for the stars. We sacrifice a marsh, a bay, a park, a lake. We sacrifice a sparrow. We trade one countdown for another.[57]

Understated here is the question: Are we next? One way to view environmentalism is that the natural world has intrinsic value for all human beings, animals, and plants. Some people, however, view this holistic view as "environmental fascism;" it nevertheless provides you with a basis for a responsible interaction with your natural world. Those who are opposed to the holistic view claim that such a view implies that grasses, for example, would be saved at the expense of the life and welfare of human beings. Do you sense an absurdity here? The point of a holistic view is that nature and human beings come together to form a "moral community" based on non-exploitation. One of the problems is the old Romantic notion that humankind is not a part of nature—that it is something above and apart from the natural world. Nothing is further from the truth. There is considerable verbiage surrounding the "Gaia-principle" which, simply put, states that the Earth is alive, a living, breathing organism existing in cooperation with all other living and breathing things. According to this view, the *biosphere*, or the totality of life on this planet influences Earth processes to sustain and advance all life. This is not a new idea by any means. Most of the ancient mythologies reveal a belief that earth is a living organism and most certainly, the ancient peoples practiced sacred rituals related to that belief. A historical view of the idea of Gaia is presented in the following chart which is based on the work of Jonathan Weiner.

THE INVESTIGATOR	THE CONTRIBUTION
William Gilbert (1540-1603)	Earth is like a magnet
Johannes Kepler (1571-1630	Earth orbits the sun elliptically
James Hutton (1726-1797)	Earth is a machine, alive & pumping, like the human body
Matthew Fontaine Maury (1806-1873)	Earth is a living being whose breath is the wind; whose blood is the sea
Vladimir Vernadsky (1863-1945)	Earth is metabolism or physiology
James Lovelock (1919-)	The Gaia Principle

If the earth is truly a living breathing organism then every time we destroy a marsh, plow up a prairie, cut down a stand of forest, or snuff out the life of a bird we are in essence killing a part of Gaia.

The question is how many wounds must she endure before she, too, dies? Wouldn't that mean the end of all life, including our own species? Environmental issues are real! And they need a strong set of ethical principles.

Background Data

Angie and her husband, Ted bought a home on one-half acres. Beautifully landscaped, the property had a three-car garage, tennis court, and an indoor swimming pool. They paid $5 million. They both loved the expansive windows, and both agreed that on a clear day you could see forever. A few weeks after being moved in, Angie began to complain that the stand of trees just below their house blocked the view. Ted, despite knowing the trees were on city-owned property, cut them down, 120 in total. The vista now offered was breathtaking, especially at sunset. Angie was delighted. One day Angie heard the gate bell ring. It was a local police officer. She pressed the button to allow the gate to swing open.

The officer had a person who represented the local environmental protection agency. They served Ted and Angie a warrant.

The Scenario

Ted and Angie immediately contacted their attorney. He did not have good news for them.

"Under state law, property owners are not guaranteed a view. Further, there are laws on the books that prohibit you from cutting down trees that are environmentally protected."

"No one said anything about that when we bought the property," Angie said. "Isn't there something we can do?"

"You have to appear in court. I will go with you, and plead you thought you had the right to cut the trees since you believed they were on your property."

"Do you think the judge will buy that?" Ted asked.

"I truthfully can't say."

The Outcome

The judge did not buy the "ignorant of the law" argument. Angie and Ted were fined $140,000 and had to buy new trees and pay to have them planted. In the meantime, since the trees would take years to mature, they had their expansive view.

INTERACTIVE TWENTY-FOUR

Directions:

Answer each of the following questions.

1. What is the primary moral issue here?

2. Is ignorance of the law ever an acceptable argument?

3. Under what circumstances do you think it is?

4. Which philosophy or philosophies could apply here?

GLOSSARY OF TERMS

ALF . . . Animal Liberation Front

Biodiversity . . . The variety of life forms found on earth

Ecocentrist . . . One who views environmental issues with cautious accommodation and a holistic point of view

EPA . . . The Environmental Protection Agency

Factory-farming . . . Large agro-business of livestock housed in large buildings which can house up to 100, 000 birds, for example.

Gaia . . . Comes from the Greek, Gaea, meaning mother goddess, earth

Gaia Hypothesis . . . A theory formulated by James Lovelock, which claims the earth, is a living organism existing in cooperation with all other living organisms.

Ideology Tensions . . . Four areas claimed to be the origin of environmental ethics: dominance vs dependence, efficiency vs equity, the present vs the future, and property rights vs responsibilities.

LUST . . . Leaking underground storage tanks

PETA . . . People for Ethical Treatment of Animals

Prairie . . . Areas too dry to sustain forest; too wet to create deserts, dominated by grasses.

Reverence for Life . . . The philosophy of Albert Schweitzer, which holds that all life, is to be revered and respected.

Sentientism . . . A philosophy that regards only living things with feelings.

Technocentrist . . . An optimistic managerialist approach to the environment; has a reductionist hierarchy.

SUGGESTED READINGS

Ackerman, Diane. The Rarest of the Rare. New York: Random House, 1995.

Capstick, Hathaway Peter. Death in a Lonely Land. New York: St. Martin's Press, 1990.

Caulfield, Catherine. In the Rainforest. Chicago: University of Chicago Press, 1991.

Colbert, Elizabeth. The Sixth Extinction: An Unnatural History. New York: Henry Holt and Company, 2014.

Leonard, Anne. The Story of Stuff: How Our Obsession with Stuff is Trashing the Planet, our Communities, our Health . . . and a Vision for Change. New York: Free Press, 2010.

Ritzer, George, and Paul Dean. Globalization: A Basic Text, Edition 2. Hoboken: John Wiley and Sons 2014.

Shnayerson, Michael. Coal River. New York: Farrar-Straus and Giroux. 2008.

Wilson, Edward O. Half-Earth: Our Planet's Fight for Life. New York: Liveright. 2016.

CHAPTER NINE
ETHICS AND THE AGE OF TECHNOLOGY

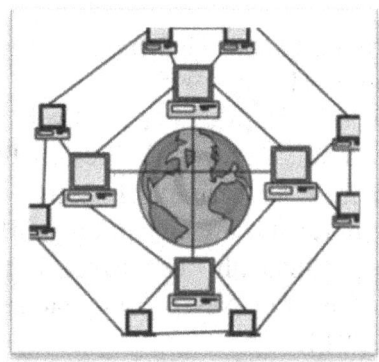

"At great human and economic costs, resources drawn from the U.S. Government, industry, and the academic community have been assembled into a collection of interconnected networks called the Internet. Begun as a vehicle for experimental network research in the mid-1970s, the Internet has become an important national infrastructure supporting an increasingly widespread multidisciplinary community of researchers ranging from computer scientists and electrical engineers to mathematicians, physicists, medical researchers, chemists, astronomers and space scientists. As is true of other common infrastructures (i.e. roads, water reservoirs, and delivery systems, and the power generation and distribution networks), there is widespread dependence on the Internet by its users for the support of day-to-day research activities. Business, as well as the private sector, have come to rely on the NET. It is no longer the domain of researchers.

The reliable operation of the Internet and the responsible use of its resources are common interests and concerns for its users, operators, and sponsors. Recent events involving the hosts on the Internet and in similar network infrastructures underscore the need to reiterate the professional responsibility every Internet user bears to colleagues and the sponsors of the system."[58]

It is also interesting to note that back in the 20th Century, the Division Advisor Panel of the National Science Foundation, Division of Network Communications Research and Infrastructure characterized as unethical five specific areas of behavior regarding the internet.[59] It is unethical for anyone to

Seek to gain unauthorized access to the resources of the Internet

Disrupt the intended use of the Internet

Waste resources through such actions

Destroy the integrity of computer-based information

Compromise the privacy of users.

Activities during the 21st Century demonstrate the concern about these five behaviors was justified. In 2016, there were nearly 4 billion Internet users. That's about 40% of the world's population. Back in 1995, the number of users was less than 1% of the world's population. These enormous figures demonstrate the huge problem faced by those who believe there should be an ethical behavior exhibited on the Internet. In 2019, there were 1,473 reported data breaches according to the report released by the *Identity Theft Resource Center*, the highest number of incidents since 2005 when tracking breaches began. Recent developments, such as the hacking of voting registration, and government officials' emails demonstrate the seriousness of the problems facing the billions of Internet users as well as government agencies and businesses worldwide. The shutdown of public libraries by hackers, the solicitation of sex online, and the general interference with the NET, availability of pornography, money-laundering schemes continue to be of concern. One of the more offensive tactics used by nefarious individuals is to capture of person's computer and to hold it for ransom. If businesses like Microsoft or AOL, or YAHOO could have their names changed by hackers, it could conceivably cost those companies millions and millions of dollars. Such a mess could happen to any business, large or small, that relies upon the Internet. Additionally, as high-tech information technologies develop, ethical issues become all the more important. Questions such as "how do you behave on the Internet," or "Should foul and profane language be allowed" become important ethical issues. Can one plan to commit a crime on the Internet? Should one be able to learn how to build a bomb by going on the Internet? Are your 'chat-rooms' private or can someone tune in? Do you really have freedom of speech on the Internet? Can you copy and print anything you want that appears on the Internet? These are just a few of the questions that plague society. Government agencies have spied on people's Internet communications. Even if you "delete" something from your computer, it can still be brought back. That information can be used against you in certain circumstances.

Recent cases of cyber-spying raise the issue of rights. One asks is "Big Brother" watching you.

The Communications Decency Act of 1996

Without a doubt, one of the more challenging areas of the NET is freedom of speech and its concurrent responsibilities. Because of concern over the availability of certain materials to persons not of legal age, the United States Congress passed legislation called, The Telecommunications Act of 1996. At the time of its signing into law, President Bill Clinton stated, "This law is truly revolutionary legislation that will bring the future to our doorsteps."

However, it is Title V of this act, which includes the provisions of the Communication Act of 1996, commonly called the *Communication Decency Act of 1996* that claimed the center of attention. An outcry rose up across the country as freedom of speech advocates claimed censorship and the libertarians and ultra-right Christian conservative groups joined in a chorus of protest; the freedom advocates claiming censorship and the ultra-right conservatives calling for stronger language in the bill. Blackouts and blue freedom of speech icons popped up on the Internet as a protest against the new legislation. The CDA of 1996 also made it illegal for a person to use telecommunications facilities for obscene, lewd, lascivious, filthy, or indecent transmission. Additionally, there was an age designation making it illegal for such transmission to anyone under 18 years old.

The American Civil Liberties Union and certain plaintiffs it represented filed suit against Janet Reno, Attorney General of the United States, asking for a temporary restraining order against the enforcement of the law.[60]

Several fundamental moral issues come into play with this legislation. First, does the government have the right to legislate morality? Should the government have that right? If it does, how is the government to decide what is moral or immoral? Then there is the question of enforcing the law. Will there be monitors in every home to listen and to watch? Has the original charge laid down by the founding fathers that the government should protect its people been carried too far? Where do you draw the line? Do you agree to some censorship for certain groups of people and not others? Will those groups be based on color, sex, age, or a combination? With the judge's decision has come some additional controversy. What does "indecent" mean? Who is to determine decency? Is picking your nose in public indecent? How about "letting air" in public? Poor taste or manners, but indecent? Is what is considered indecent in Alabama the same for Alaska? Instead of clarifying issues, all that has been achieved is mass confusion over intent.

CASE STUDY 1.18 - (The REDDINGS)

Background Data:

Mike and Jennifer Redding ran an online bulletin board service featuring explicit images of bestiality, sadomasochism, and other sexual fetishes.

A United States postal inspector downloaded their explicit material. The inspector lived in Rome, TN; the Reddings lived in California.

The convicted couple appealed their case. The Sixth Circuit Court of Appeals in Cincinnati, Ohio, however, upheld their convictions.

Note these two key points: The Reddings were tried in Rome because that's where the postal inspector downloaded their explicit material from their bulletin board. Second, a 1973 U.S. Supreme Court ruling (413 U.S. 15 Miller v California) allowed the regulation of obscenity based on the notion of "community standards." But until the Reddings' trial, that ruling had not been applied specifically to the material on an online service in a city in which the material was received, rather than at the site of its creation.

Two statements about this case[61] are of interest: The first, b Mike Godwin of the Electronic Frontier Foundation. He said, "What happens is this, the most conservative jurisdictions in the country can now dictate standards for the rest of the country." The second statement by Stephen Bates of the Annenberg Washington Projects (a communications think-tank): "You might as well say that pornography should be judged by the worldwide community of pornographers. The law is geographic in how it looks at jurisdictions, boundaries, and everything else. That is not going to change just because a new technology comes along."

INTERACTIVE TWENTY-FIVE

Directions:

Go to Appendix Number Two and read the material on how to create a case study. Using that information, create a case study using the above material. You may add your own dialogue, add characters, and change the sequence of events. Be sure your case study reflects one of the philosophies discussed in this book.

We need to remember responsible Internet behavior is not localized. It is worldwide. The Association for Computing Machinery (ACM), for example, has a most impressive code of professional conduct. It contains a section called "General Moral Imperatives" which functions as a set of commandments. They are worthy of being repeated here.

Contribute to society and human well-being
Avoid harm to others
Be honest and trustworthy
Be fair and take action not to discriminate
Honor property rights including copyrights and patents

Give proper credit for intellectual property
Respect the privacy of others, and
Honor confidentiality

The ACM is not the only source for promoting appropriate Internet usage. The Canadian Information Processing Society (CIPS) in its Code expects its membership to protect the public interest and strive to promote understanding of information processing and its applications. From the Computer Ethics Institute comes the "Ten Commandments of Computer Ethics" which includes consideration and respect for your fellow humans." Colleges and universities with computer services available to their students face multiple challenges. Public libraries with free public access to the Internet are equally challenged. Should they censor or adhere to freedom of speech and privacy principles? A student in Informatics at the University of Hamburg writes in his *Oath of Information*, "I will respect the human rights, the privacy of individuals, and the democratic freedom of information."[62] The Computer Society of Zimbabwe Code of Professional Conduct expects its members to "respect the confidentially of client information." One final example: The Australian Computer Society's Code of Ethics includes statements that embrace honesty, professional development, and the quality of life.

The keywords, listed in the box below, from each of these ethical statements provide an interesting insight into what is considered acceptable behavior.

> *Human well being*
> *Honesty*
> *Trustworthiness*
> *Fairness*
> *Respect and honor*
> *Professional development*
> *Quality of life*

Embodied in these few key words are several of the major concepts of a theory of ethics called *Humanitarian Ethics*. Simply put, Humanitarian Ethics emphasizes the human condition worldwide and without distinctions of any kind. It propagates human potential, human responsibility, neutrality in times of suffering and need, and transformation. By transformation, the Humanitarians want to build institutions and public attitudes that respond to all peoples and their direct needs. Acceptable social behavior is not just for the users of the Internet. It should be for all aspects of society.

Despite these admirable goals, there remain issues of confidentiality and property rights. Imbedded in various codes of ethics is a respect for the property rights of others. But what constitutes property rights? Are electronic correspondences you have with your priest, pastor, or rabbi your property? What about faxes and emails to your attorney? Are these types of correspondences your property and therefore held inviolate? Is your name, address your property, and can they be transmitted electronically to telemarketing businesses, to businesses that compile mailing lists and in turn sell them to others? Because of a concern for confidentiality and privacy, the Internal Revenue Service canceled plans to start a new electronic tax-filing system after discovering serious flaws that jeopardized the security of taxpayer information. This was the Cyberfile System and contained at least seventeen weaknesses that were subject to attack.

Do charities have the right to share your name and address with other charities? Are your medical records, for example, your property or do they belong to your doctor? Once those medical records are electronically sent to another physician, clinic, or hospital are they fair game for cyber thieves? Are medical facilities and health insurance companies responsible for the confidentiality of your records? Upon what is this assumed confidentiality based? The idea of your personal health as an area of confidentiality dates back to the 4th Century, B. C. E., and the Oath of Hippocrates.

Whatsoever things I see or hear concerning the life of men, in my attendance on the sick or even apart thereon, which ought not be noised abroad, I will keep silence thereon, counting such things to be as sacred secrets. Hippocrates.

The Issue of Electronic Medical Records

Mark Totenberg of Epic.Org (Electronic Privacy Information Center Organization) states, "No information is more sensitive or potentially more stigmatizing than personal health records. At the same time, medical data have enormous value to researchers and health care provides, offering insight for the epidemiologist and quantitative assessment of health care effectiveness. Striking this balance is not an easy task."[63] Of concern are the health database organizations, which have access to person-identifiable health care data outside of the health care setting. The information gathered by these organizations is released to the public in the form of studies about health providers and other health care issues. Even though persons are not identified in these public released reports, those who compile the baseline data do have that information. This is a cause for concern.

Yet, over time, several exceptions to this expected confidentiality have emerged; namely, in the following areas: statutory requirements requiring the notification of abortions, births, some deaths, certain diseases, non-accidental injuries (child abuse, for example), and fitness to drive. Do you feel you agree to have your records released because you have sought treatment? Can you demand that your records not be kept on a computer system? There may be some justification for not having such records placed on a computer if you are a person who might be in danger if your identity and medical records could become now through a cyber-attack and used by some unscrupulous person or persons.

A banker, for example, who sits on a health commission, has access to a list of all the patients in his state who have been diagnosed with cancer. Crosschecking that list with his list of banking clients, he determined with of those clients had cancer and call in all of their loans. Unscrupulous is a mild term for such potential behavior. As with other areas, the possibility of your records being disclosed depends primarily on two factors: its value and the number of people who have access to it. The United States Government Office of Technology Assessment has confirmed that the main threat to the privacy of your medical records in computerized clinical record systems come from insiders rather than outsiders.

Property and Its Protection

John Perry Barlow in "The Economy of Ideas"[64]stated that in cyberspace "an immense, unsolved conundrum has remained at the root of nearly every legal, ethical, governmental, and social vexation to be found in the Virtual World."[65] According to Mr. Barlow, that conundrum is what to do with the digitized property. Technology is now so advanced that if your ideas (if recorded), materials you have created can be instantly copied, reproduced, transmitted, and distributed worldwide at no benefit to you. In other words, you receive no credit or money for your creative efforts. With the advent of social groups (Twitter, Facebook, Pinterest, YouTube, Snapchat, and Instagram), and the many websites that post articles and photos it is all too easy to download someone else's work and use it. Creations can be anything, which can be transmitted via the Internet—a joke you makeup, a recipe, lyrics for a song, a cartoon, and a poem you composed for a friend, fractals, or a new language. Consider the artwork you design for your "home page" on your website. Is that fair game for copying? The late author-philosopher Ayn Rand vehemently denied that anyone had rights to your creative efforts. Intellectual property law has become a major issue in the world of instant communication.

Infringements of copyright have taken place around the world. Records, videos, films, as well as computer software, have illegally been copied and distributed at great profits to everyone but the creators of those works. Barlow reminds us of a most significant fact, yet a detail that is all too often overlooked: "Notions of property, value, ownership, and the nature of wealth itself are changing more fundamentally than at any time since the Sumerians first poked cuneiform into a wet call and called it 'stored grain.'"[66] To demonstrate the truth of the Barlow statements just examine the number of items you can now purchase over the NET with just a number. Is that number real property?

Three aspects of information are identified by Barlow provide a clue as to the role of ethics in modern technology.

Information is an activity (something that happens)

Information is a life form (comes into being, changes, expands)

Information is a relationship (connects, evolves, involves)

Assume for a moment that these three roles are true. Each implies an interaction; interaction involves behavior and behavior implies acceptable or unacceptable, and that's ethics. Barlow asserts that the protection of your intellectual property rights will rely more on ethics than on law. Do you agree?

Simon Rogerson and Terrell Ward Bynum in "Cyberspace: The Ethical Frontier"[67] suggest three specific areas of focus if society is to survive the information technologies revolution:

1. Ethical development- involves the consideration of the way information systems redeveloped, and which must now include societal and ethical considerations as well as economic ones

2. Ethical technology-involves a concern about the actual technologies used to build systems; the way such systems should be constructed.

3. Ethical application-involves a concern for an ethically sensitive application of technology

strategies; the game plan or the how-to of technology.

Rogerson and Bynum state, "Computer ethics, however, should be the concern of everyone, not simply computer professionals. The future of society and the advancement of human values are too important to be left simply to technologists. Governments, public policymakers, organizations, and private citizens must all take an interest and make their contributions."[68] Within this context, Rogerson and Bynum raise some important ethical questions:

What will happen to human relationships and the community when most human activities are carried on in cyberspace from one's home?

Whose laws will apply in cyberspace when hundreds of countries are incorporated into the global network?

Will the poor be disenfranchised, cut off from job opportunities, education, entertainment, medical care, shopping, voting because they cannot afford a connection to the Internet and the equipment to do it?

CASE STUDY 1.19 - (TRICKY DICK

Background Data:

Kay Snow, the sales manager for one of 28 electronic stores, has managed her present store for eighteen months. She and her staff have been working very hard to increase their sales. After several weeks of hard work, Kay and her staff no only met the sales goal but went over the top, giving her store the highest sales gain in her district.

Kay and her fellow employees were ecstatic when they reported their final numbers. They eagerly looked forward to a raise for a job well done.

Richard Thomson, the district sales manager, has a bad reputation when it comes to fair play with those who work under him. His primary goal is to look out for Richard.

A district sales manager must meet three criteria for promotion to a regional manager. First, all stores need to show positive month-to-month sales gain for two years in a row. Second, all stores had to show a positive net profit with the same time parameters, and third, stores in the district had to be number one or number two in terms of credit card sales on a month-to-month and yearly basis. Richard wanted to be a regional sales manager.

The Scenario:

Kay Snow suppressed her impulse to light up a cigarette as she looked around the back room of the electronics specialty store. Though she had quit smoking some time ago, a disturbing phone call from her district manager triggered the urge for a nicotine fix.

Pacing the floor she muttered, "Tricky Dick strikes again," and gave an empty electronics box a swift kick. Richard Thompson had told her that he was transferring $4,000 out of her sales to another store that was short of its sales goals. In that way, he could claim a first 100 percent district-wide sales gain.

"No nothing, no discussion, just bam," Kay thought. She had tried to reason with Richard, but he would have none of it. "I can't believe this is happening."

For Kay, this was just not right. It violated the spirit of the incentive program, destroyed store moral. She sat down on a box, took off her shoe, and rubbed her kicking foot. It hurt. "Do I have a responsibility here without endangering my own position? There must be something I can do about Richard. And what am I to tell my sales team?"

INTERACTIVE TWENTY-SIX

Directions

Assume you are Kay Snow. Finish the scenario; include dialogue and an ending. Have Kay answer her own questions. Once you have the storyline completed, do each of the following:
Identify the primary moral issue
Identify the primary moral principle
List three alternatives for Kay
Identify your personal choice of those alternatives and justify your choice,
Identify the ethical theory involved in this case. Justify your choice.

Finally, answer these questions. Do Kay's sales representatives have a right to demand full commissions for the sales they generated? Do you think this would be a legal issue? Would this be a Union issue? If you don't know, do some research.[69]

***

The Cell Phone brings New Ethical Issues

Concern about privacy and security on the Internet is but one area in which violations can and do take place. The cell phone comes with its own set of moral baggage. As with the NET, the cell phone was a toy and playground for a small number of people. Created by Martin Cooper in 1973, the cell phone changed the way people lived probably more so than the Internet. Business people, professionals, parents, children, college students, housewives, singles, retired have all bought into the questionable reality that cell phones are a necessity. New phones have a wide range of technologies available such as taking photos, texting, appointment calendars, call back, call forwarding, caller id.

Cell phones open up additional possibilities for the invasion of privacy, bullying, sex trafficking, pornography, money laundering, and drug dealing. Hackers can map any phone call placed within your broadcast area. Because vehicles move from one area to another, cell phone messages are transferred from one cell to another. Such call can and movements can be traced. You see examples of this on any number of television programs. If an overzealous law enforcement agency systematically did this, wouldn't your civil rights be violated? What about your right to privacy?

Another and perhaps more fundamental issue with the massive use of cell phones and the games that can be played on them is that it develops anti-social skills. You have seen a young couple seated in a restaurant totally absorbed in their cell phone texting or games. How does this develop positive social interaction? On the other hand, some socialist claims the cell phone has brought families closer together. In today's world, there is no question that they bring a positive safety factor. At the same time, one has to wonder about all the cell phones being used to photo law enforcement operations. There is no question that they have brought a much-needed focus to that area.

SUGGESTED READINGS

Ermann, William, MD & C. Gutierrez, Eds. **Computer Ethics and Society**. New York: Oxford University Press, 1990

Forester, T. & P. Morrison. Computer Ethics: Cautionary Tales and Ethical Dilemmas in Computing. Cambridge: MIT Press, 1994

Hafner, Katie & John Markoff. **Cyberpunk: Outlaws and Hackers on the Computer Frontier**. New York: Simon & Schuster, 1991.

Jacky, J. "Programmed for disaster: Software Errors That Imperil Lives," *The Sciences. Sept/Oct 1989.*

Kolb, Liz." Cell Phones in the Classroom-A Practical Guide for Educators." International Society for Technology in Education. 2011.

Johnson, Deborah G. **Computer Ethics, 4th Ed.** New York: Parsons, 2009.

Johnson, Douglas W. **Computer Ethics: A Guide to a New Age**. Elgin: The Brethren Press, 1984.

Parker, D. & B.S. Swope & B. N. Baker. **Ethical Conflicts in Information and Computer Science, Technology, and Business**. Wellesley. QED Information Services, 1990.

Plotkin, Robert. **Computer Ethics, Computer, Internet, and Society**. New York: Facts On File, Inc. 2011.

Roberts, James A., Luc Honore Peinji Yaya & Chris Manolis. "The Invisible Addiction: Cellphone Activities and Addiction among Male and Female College Students." Journal of Behavioral Addictions. Published online, Aug. 26, 2014.

Shinder, Deb. "Ethical Issues for IT Professionals," *Computer World*, August 2, 2005.

Slatalla, Mihelle & Joshua Quttner. **Masters of deception: The Gang that ruled Cyberspace.** New York: Harper Collins Publishers, 1995.

Sterling, Bruce. The Hacker Crackdown: Law and Disorder on the Electronic Frontier. New York: Bantam Books, 1992.

CHAPTER TEN
A COMPROMISE OF SORTS

With widely divergent ethical theories available, which one do you choose as the basis for your personal moral behavior? Can you select a single ethic and have it be applicable to all aspects of your life? Each ethical theory has its strong and weak points, even the much-revered Golden Rule. Lawrence M. Hinman[70] suggests that what is needed is a greater degree of integration of the personal element in moral life. He calls for a "reshaping" of ethical theory. However, can you reshape ethical theory and have it remain universal? Without the quality of universality, any ethical system would be unattainable. If you adhere to one moral system and your friend to another, how can you ever absolve any issues? And in any relationship, there are issues. Does it, after all, simply boil down to your choice—what you believe? In this chapter, two approaches to contemporary ethics will be examined; each is an attempt at compromise. The first suggested compromise is Humanitarian Ethics offered by Jacques P. Thiroux and the second compromise, Idealist Ethics is offered by Amit Goswami.

Humanitarian Ethics:

Thiroux[71] identifies five essential characteristics of a moral system if it is to be tenable.

A moral system should be rationally based; yet, not exclude emotion

It should be logically consistent; yet, not inflexible

It should be applicable on a universal level as well as to particular persons and situations

It should be teachable

It should provide a basis for resolving conflicts among human beings, duties, and obligations.

Several theories center on absolutes and have a limited notion of freedom. Absolute means without exception. Some of the limitations on your freedom are legal, economic, and social; others are moral in nature. Thiroux assumes you understand these restrictions imposed on your personal freedom. As he outlines in his Humanitarian Ethics, his first four principles will show themselves to be restrictive of your freedom. For example, the necessity of preserving and protecting human life precludes your freedom to kill someone just because you do not like that individual's eyes. One of the key elements in Humanitarian Ethics is that of personal action or involvement. Note that each of his five principles includes some form of action.

Thiroux begins his theory by proposing five major principles. *The First Principle*, The Value of Life Principle, states, "Human beings should revere life and accept death." The idea of reverence for life and the acceptance of the inevitability of death is not a new concept. It is traceable to antiquity. It is the *leitmotif* in the ancient Sumerian myth, "The Epic of Gilgamesh," which reveals Gilgamesh's refusal to accept the inevitably of his death. It was written some 1300 years before Homer's two great literary works, *The Iliad* and *The Odyssey*. The idea for the reverence for life is found in Samuel Taylor Coleridge's *The Rime of the Ancient Mariner*. Coleridge created a new language to express Romantic ideals, had his ancient mariner learn that it is necessary to respect all life, even the lowest slimy creatures of the sea. Modern science fiction often addresses the question of respect and reverence. In the 1980's television series, *Voyager*, Captain Janeway is genuinely concerned about respecting other civilizations and life forms

Nearly every culture reflects some concern for the preservation and protection of human life—even the famous IK tribe of Africa, despite its being called "loveless." Even though the idea is an old one, it does not detract from Thiroux's restatement of it. The point to understand is that life is the **basic** possession. And as such, it is certainly common to all human beings. Does this make this principle an absolute? Yes, it does! It is the first principle and everything else in Humanitarian Ethics is pinioned to it. It is sacrosanct! It appears many in current society no longer believe in this principle with the daily shootings and stabbings that are occurring. Do you feel our society no longer places a high value on life?

The Second Principle, "The Principle of Goodness and Rightness," holds that all persons should strive to be good and should attempt to carry out right actions. Here, Thiroux suggests human beings should promote goodness over badness as well as do good themselves. You should do no badness, harm to others, or be the cause of it. Is this not Aristotle's character ethics? Thiroux goes one-step further. He states human beings should prevent badness or harm which in turn opens the larger question of involvement and action—the very issue with which the early Romantics struggled and failed to resolve. Viewing the crime situation in the United States, do you think the Second Principle has an application? The underlying assumption of this Principle is that moral persons lead good lives and perform right actions. Proof of this is displayed in happiness, pleasure, personal harmony, and excellence in life. Of course, not everyone can be an Albert Schweitzer, Mahatma Gandhi, Martin Luther King Tom Dooley, or Mother Teresa. However, each of you may choose to do good in your own way as these notable persons have. Isn't that what this Principle is all about—doing good? It is being involved in life in a positive, contributing, and nurturing way. It is action!

The Third Principle called "The Principle of Justice and Fairness" is concerned with the distribution of good and bad. It is concerned with the idea that a fair basis exists for that distribution. You should treat others justly and fairly not because what you can gain by doing so, but because it is the right thing to do. Notice the word "treat," is an action word and demands involvement. According to Thiroux, it is not enough to try to distribute justice and fairness—a real effort must be made to distribute their benefits. Doesn't this principle involve consequentialism? Yet, can you also see that there is room for capital punishment here? Does the Principle of Justice and Fairness have an application to social programs? Does it provide a basis for awarding scholarships and grants to college students? Would the notion of ethnic quotas and affirmative action find a place within this principle? Principle Three involves more than dividing a pie equally into a predetermined number of pieces. Other factors come into play. Can standards be established that could apply to justice and fairness in the workplace, in the legal and social place? A large number of existing ethical codes demonstrate the numerous attempts at creating such standards. Nearly every professional and occupational career has a code of ethics for those who practice in them. It has been stated that our society is rich in everything but justice. Recent court cases, police usurpation of civil rights, police shooting of unarmed individuals, and hacking of people's personal email lend credence to such experiences. Do you feel there is a lack of justice in your world? If you do, what actions are you willing to take to improve it?

The Fourth Principle, "The Principle of Truth Telling and Honesty," is absolutely essential for any moral theory; it is also absolutely essential for you if you are to have any meaningful relationships. This is probably the most difficult of the five principles to live by; the reason being your vulnerability when it comes to personal relationships. Everyone is vulnerable, yet Dr. Leo Buscaglia tells you that unless you are willing to take risks you gain nothing and every personal encounter is a risk. Can you imagine a relationship lasting if it is built upon lies and deceit? Have you been hurt because this principle was lacking or because it had been violated? Not only does the principle of truth-telling and honesty have relevance to you personally, but it also applies to businesses and governments as well. Shouldn't world treaties be based upon trust—truthfulness being the building block of that trust?

Do you believe that it is always necessary to tell the truth? Is it always best to tell the truth? Are there circumstances when not telling the truth might be acceptable, if not preferable; that it might be kinder and gentler not to tell the truth? Should a doctor, for example, tell a patient that she is terminally ill? If that doctor tells the patient that she is terminally ill, isn't that doctor denying her hope? What do you say to a sick person who is a hospital? Do you tell them they look great when the patient and you both know it is not true? Your younger brother or sister is at home alone. The telephone rings; it's a stranger who wants to know if anyone else is at home. Should your sibling tell the truth or should he or she lie? Fortunately, Thiroux leaves the door open to circumstances. And since he does, isn't that relativism? If you are in a relationship, do you tell that person everything about your previous relationships? Or do you build trust and truth-telling within your present relationship? Not everyone agrees you should tell all. What do you think? Wouldn't you want to know if someone with whom you might be intimate has AIDS? So, what do you do; ask them for a recent medical report?

The Fifth Principle called "The Principle of Individual Freedom" provides the flexibility necessary in an ethical system. You must be free to choose your ways and means of being moral within the framework of the first four principles proposed by Thiroux or they will have no relevancy. Several limiting factors to our freedom have been mentioned here and other chapters. Thiroux points out that the first four principles unto themselves limit personal freedom. If you tell the truth, you cannot be telling a lie at the same time. If you have a reverence for life, you don't commit murder.

The basis for any freedom is choice. Deny choice and you have no freedom. Even the simplest act of choosing the clothes you wore today involves freedom of choice. Admittedly, certain groups of determinists could argue that you were preconditioned to select what you wore, but such argumentation still begs the issue. Why did you choose what you did on the day you did? Because you wanted to and that is freedom!

CASE STUDY 1.20 - (PHARMACEUTICAL VS THE FDA)

Background Data

A major pharmaceutical company has placed on the market a new version of a drug for sufferers of asthma at a cost of $90.00 a bottle.

The Food and Drug Administration has ordered the company to change its formula because tests on laboratory animals have shown that its main ingredient caused cancer. In compliance, the company reformulated its asthma medication and shipped it to drug stores under a new name. It did not reveal that it contained the same ingredients found in cough remedies selling for a mere $5 a bottle.

The Scenario

The American Consumer Advocacy Council filed suit against the pharmaceutical company claiming it "basically perpetrated a fraud on the public." In court, Margie Alan, attorney for the pharmaceutical, made the following statement:

"Our responsibility [the company's] has been to provide the best possible drug available for the treatment of asthma and other breathing disorders. We have done that. Our product has met the requirements of the Food and Drug Administration. We have taken great care in repackaging our product and in providing instructions to doctors that this is not the old formula, but a new one."

Attorney Diane Smithfield, for the ACAC, replied

"But you have not informed the medical profession or the public that your product is basically the same drug that can be had in a nationally known cough syrup, that there is nothing special about this new medication that makes it more effective. You have made the public think this is a new drug simply by changing the name of the old one when in reality all you did was remove an ingredient. That's a fraud, no matter how you spell it."

"Despite what you claim, we have complied with every federal requirement," Margie Alan said.

"No, all you have done is sell this product like you would a bar of soap—in new packaging, with a label saying it's a new and improved product," Smithfield replied.

The sitting judge interrupted. "What is the benefit over the ordinary drugs now available over the counter?"

But before Alan could answer, Diane Smithfield responded. "The one benefit this drug has for its users is it's covered by their health insurance; whereas, over-the-counter drugs are not."

"Your honor, if you force us to withdraw this product after the millions and millions of dollars we have spent in research, promotion, and repackaging we'll go bankrupt. We simply cannot suffer such a loss. Thousands of people will be out of work. You will have put us out of business," pleaded Margie Alan

INTERACTIVE TWENTY-SEVEN
Directions:

Answer each of these questions.

Using Thiroux's "Humanitarian Ethics," which principle(s) does this case violate.

Does the right to make a profit alter the need for truthfulness and honesty, especially when jobs are at risk? Why or why not?

How would you apply Thiroux's Third Principle if you were the hearing judge? Be specific in your answer.

Immanuel Kant used a story about a shopkeeper to illustrate the honesty in business principle. Find this example, and use it in this case.

Some Problems with Humanitarian Ethics

As with other ethical theories, Thiroux's Humanitarian Ethics has its share of problems. "The Principle of Goodness and Rightness," the second Thiroux principle, implies certain identifying characteristics that may raise serious questions. Among these characteristics is the notion that a moral person is a good person. Second, a good person will enjoy happiness, pleasure, excellence, personal harmony, a degree of creativity, and a general lack of pain. How do you define these words: happiness, pleasure, excellence, personal harmony? Are they to be defined only by particular individuals? If so, then what happens if your happiness and/or pleasure interfere with another's?

The issue involved here is that individual freedom—your freedom to define what constitutes your happiness, pleasure, and harmony. Even Aristotle, as brilliant as he was, is not much help here. His definition of happiness has been the center of controversy for years. Thiroux, recognizing this problem, still believes there are some *goods* common to everyone and everyone can agree on those. Among these *goods* are life, consciousness, love, and self-expression. Do you agree that these goods are common to all people? What about those "good" people who have a life filled with turmoil, pain, and suffering. Would the "Book of Job" be helpful here?

A second problem revolves around "The Principle of Justice and Fairness." Who is to determine what is fair, A judge, religious leaders, professors, parents, or you? What if everyone in a society does not believe justice and fairness have been served? There are many examples in history and in present-day that demonstrate that not everyone believes justice and fairness exist. Many black citizens in the United States feel a lack as do the Japanese Americans that were incarcerated during World War Two. Do you apply the Utilitarian principle of "the greater good for the greatest number of people" in metering out justice? What role does W. D. Ross' "prima facie duties" play in determining justice and fairness? Who decides what is an equal distribution of the benefits of being good? On the other hand, who decides what the benefits are?

"The Principle of Truth Telling and Honesty" also presents problems. How do you know if someone is telling the truth? Even lie detector machines have been called into question. How do you know if someone is honest? Are these not issues of trust? Do you automatically trust someone or do they have to earn it? How you earn trust if you have been caught not telling the truth? Are you justified in questioning everyone about everything they say or do? If you do, you will soon be friendless. As with the other Thiroux principles, personal judgment comes into play. Remember, personal judgment can be wrong.

The biggest problem area, secondly only to Truth Telling and Honesty, probably is within "The Principle of Individual Freedom." In any modern ethical belief system, flexibility seems to be a crucial element. But how much flexibility is the question? As much flexibility as the weather changes? Wouldn't that lead to open conflict and a general chaotic state of affairs? Society's rules called laws, and rules of religious systems called dogmas, place limitations of flexibility. If laws and religious dogmas restrict you, do you demand exceptions so that you can fulfill your own need for flexibility? "Buckle-up" is a law in all fifty states.

Yet, you feel the seat belt around your body impedes your personal freedom. Do you not buckle-up and violate the law? What if you have a passenger, neither of you uses the seat belts, and you have an accident. Your passenger is seriously injured. Are you morally accountable? You can be legally held responsible, but can you morally claim your right to individual freedom as an excuse from that accountability? No, you cannot.

Another problem area is priority. Is there any way—a practical way—to determine how to prioritize your moral principles? Unlike W. D. Ross, Thiroux attempts to provide a practical approach to prioritizing your moral principles. He suggests that your moral principles may be prioritized in a general way and then, in a particular way. In the general way, which he calls *logical priority*, that is, priority based on logic and empirical evidence. Into this category are placed two principles: "The Value of Life Principle," and "The Principle of Goodness and Rightness." The *particular priority* category identifies priorities by the actual situation or context in which your moral decisions and actions occur. The remaining three principles fall under this category: "The Principle of Justice and Fairness," "The Principle of Telling the Truth and Honesty," and "The Principle of Freedom." A sort of a compromise is reached, that is, room for circumstance, situation, time, and place is made within the context of universal principles.

Most likely, an absolutist would find this approach unacceptable; the consequentialist would if he could determine that the greatest good had been accomplished for the greatest number. In the final analysis, Thiroux makes an appeal for common sense in dealing with your moral acts and decisions, and therein, is the real crux of the problem. Somewhere at some time, you have been taken to task for not using "common sense." Can an acceptable definition of "common sense" be arrived at? The words from the Latin come to mind, *sēus commūs*, meaning "common feelings of humanity." Implied is the additional meaning of "native good judgment." You be the judge. Thiroux is a compromise of sorts between the extremes of absolutism and relativism. Moral acts and decisions do not exist in the abstract; they occur in the reality of your everyday existence involving you in particular situations and beliefs. These beliefs involve you with particular people—personally.

INTERACTIVE TWENTY-EIGHT

Directions:

Arrange Thiroux's five principles in terms of their importance to you, that is, their priority. Which would you list first?

Decide which of the following issues would be placed in the Logical Category and which would be placed in the Particular Category of Thiroux's Humanitarian Ethics. Us the letters LC (Logical Category) and PC (Particular Category) next to the number of each of the following to indicate your choice.

Abortion

Pulling the plug on a terminally ill person

Telling your date that you have to break the date because of a sick friend when you don't have a sick friend

Playing your music late at night so loudly that it disturbs your apartment neighbors who have to get up early to go to work

Claiming you did more work than you did, thus causing another employee to lose his/her job.

INTERACTIVE TWENTY-NINE

Directions:

Create a case study to illustrate one of Thiroux's principles. Follow the procedures for developing a case study outlined in Appendix Two Be sure you identify which of the five principles you are using.

CASE STUDY 1.21 (ED VS J.A.)

Background Data

Ed worked for a fast-food restaurant chain as a district supervisor. He had worked for the company since he graduated from high school. He is now 35 years old, married, and childless. His wife, Helen, is a pretty woman who does not work outside of the home. She spends her time doing things for local charities.

Tina is the manager of one of the six restaurants Ed supervises. She is unmarried, attractive, and has a college degree in restaurant management. She has worked for the company for five years.

Ed and Tina have been having an affair. When he travels the sixty miles to visit her restaurant, he arranges to have a room at a local motel. They send each other amorous whispered messages via their voice mail.

J. A. Brossard, the owner of the six franchised restaurants, is their boss. He is sixty years old, married, and the grandfather of two.

The Scenario

J.A., as he was called began to monitor Ed's voice mail after he accidentally heard one of the whispered love messages. He recognized Tina's voice. He then visited each of his six stores, so as not to arouse suspicion, and while at Tina's store, J.A. checked her voice mail. He heard Ed's voice telling Tina to be ready for him next week. J.A. was furious.

As J.A. was driving home he muttered to himself, "Not going to have my employees caring on like that. And to think, Ed's a married man. Nice little woman, he's got for a wife, too. How's that old saying go, "the wife is the last to know."

The next day, J.A. recorded the voice messages, called Helen, Ed's wife, and asked her to meet him at another restaurant in town. Helen agreed, no knowing the reason for the meeting. At the restaurant, J.A. played the tape for Helen. She was devastated, and sure others in the restaurant heard. Crying, she got up and ran out the door.

The following day, J.A. fired Ed, but not Tina. Ed could not believe his boss and mentor had stooped so low as to listen to and record his voice mail.

Post Script[72]

Ed and Helen worked out the issues and remained together as husband and wife. Both sued J.A. Brossard and the mother company of his franchise. Each asked for one million dollars. The couple claimed that Brossard violated their privacy rights guaranteed them by federal law and that he intentionally inflicted emotional anguish and embarrassment on both of them. Note that nothing was said about the unfairness of firing Ed and not Tina.

INTERACTIVE THIRTY

Directions:

Answer each of the following questions.
Does Humanitarian Ethics apply to Case 1.21? If so, how; if not, which theory does?
What is the primary moral issue in this case?
What is the primary moral principle in this case?
On what basis might you justify J. A. Brossard's behavior? Do you think he deliberately "inflicted harm on Ed and Helen? Support your opinion with examples from the case.
Can one's behavior ever be justified? How? For what reason(s)?

An Idealist Theory of Ethics:

Dr. Amit Goswami in "An Idealist Theory of Ethics"[73] proposes a new ethical theory as well as raising several provocative questions in terms of modern ethical values. The late Joseph Campbell, believing there was a malaise in America's value system, wrote, "With our old mythologically founded taboos unsettled by our modern sciences, there is everywhere in the civilized world a rapidly rising incidence of vice and crime, mental disorders, suicides, and dope addictions, shattered homes, impudent children, violence, murder, and despair."[74]

Agreeing with Campbell, Goswami asks, "Can we restore values and ethics that are free of dogma? Can we understand values and ethics stripped of their mythological base?"[75] He believes you can and you are to find a new basis in what he calls "an idealist theory of ethics," one based on certain fundamental scientific principles found in quantum physics. Goswami, however, is not the first to turn to science in an attempt to prove or illustrate philosophical concepts. Non-determinists, for example, allude to the Heisenberg experiments in quantum physics to prove human beings are free. Goswami contends freedom fundamental in a quantum world view is fundamental to ethics also.

At this point, it is helpful to summarize some of the main points Dr. Goswami makes about quantum physics.[76]

Quantum objects develop as a multifaceted wave until human observation collapses them into one-faceted particles

Such collapses are discontinuous and acausal

This signifies a new beginning

Photons have been found to influence one another at a distance without any exchange of signals through space-time, and thus, indicating their nonlocal interconnectedness.

If, and it is a big if, mind-objects are quantum objects, then beyond human ego separateness, there could be nonlocal connections. Nonlocality is the principle that something can be affected in the absence of a local cause. An excellent example of nonlocality is offered by Danah Zohar.[77] Twins, separated at birth, living in different parts of the world and never having communicated with one another, dress the same way, use the same nickname, have the same profession, and marry blonde-haired women with the same first name are affected by the absence of a local cause—their nonlocality. Some would call this synchrony. You certainly could ask if this is not similar to the "oneness" concept so highly apprized by the early Greeks. The answer would be yes. What is strongly suggested, here, is that each of you is connected to the other—thus, making the concept of all of you being brothers and sisters, true.

Further, if such nonlocal consecutiveness is possible, then human beings would not exist in separateness one from another; they would, much as are the photons, be connected. Since such a connectedness does exist, in Goswami's Idealist Theory, there is an implied harmonious relationship. Goswami urges you to accept the notion of inseparability as an established principle. He does not, interestingly enough, put down your traditional spiritual-religious heritage—one which claims "unity in diversity."

Goswami believes that such a heritage acts as a bridge to connect scientific and philosophical idealism. Idealism may be defined as an attempt to account for all objects in nature and experiences as representations of the mind. (For additional discussion of Idealism see Plat, George Berkeley, Hegel, and F. H. Bradley) Goswami states, "The new ethics will not be calcified by ritual belief systems; instead, it will flow meaningfully from the human being's pursuit of "inner" creativity—an urge for the transformation of being."[78] Next, he calls for an acceptance of the world that is **you** on a most personal level. Sound almost existentialist, doesn't it?

Transcendence[79] another important aspect of Idealist Ethics poses no problem with the concept of nonlocal correlations just as in quantum physics there is no problem with nonlocal domains. In quantum physics observations of quantum objects cause them to collapse. Goswami maintains this is also true if you accept the notion that mental objects are collapsed by your consciousness from many-faceted waves into one-facet particles in your awareness—your mind-field.[80]

In Idealist Ethics, according to Dr. Goswami, you have the inherent privilege to act in a quantum modality—that is, with freedom of choice and creativity. At the same time, as you acknowledge your freedom of choice and creativity you also acknowledge your responsibility for those choices and acts of creativity. Goswami drops a bombshell.

He asks, "Is the purpose of idealist ethics then, to define "good" choices as opposed to "bad" choices, to categorize right and wrong better than realist ethics?" [81] Can't you ask that same question of every ethical system? Is that what ethics is all about? The difference between good/bad choices? Without question, the role of morality is the determination of rightness/goodness and wrongness//badness. Implied here, is the notion that you are responsible for your moral behavior, not some outside force. If indeed, humans operate on a quantum modality, then they do make choices. But why are some choices good, others being wrong or bad? Do such choices depend on time, place, and circumstance? Isn't this rationalism or consequentialism? The problem arises, for most people, when they attempt to impose the application of general ethical principles on too varied circumstances. Quantum modality accommodates time, place, and circumstance; change, fluctuation, and chaos.

In an idealist theory of ethics what constitutes "sin"? Does it mean 'thou shalt not' of Christianity? Does it mean not following the Eight-fold Path of Buddhism? Traditional religious training or background does not provide you with an answer. In idealist ethics, which embraces a quantum view, sin means to completely "fossilize self or others in classical functioning, to block one's own or another's access to the quantum modality and the manifestation of freedom and creativity. (That such access provides.)[82] The fundamental idealist ethical principle may be stated as "the preservation and enhancement of our own and other's access to the quantum modality—to the quantum level of being (which includes both freedom and creativity).[83] In an Idealist Ethics, which encompasses a quantum modality, you should adhere to the following.

Avoid preconceived answers

Have creative as your goal

Be open to possibilities without taking shortcuts, and

Embrace uncertainty and doubt as requisites for your creativity.

CASE STUDY 1.22 (JOE)

Background Data:

Joe, a thirty-eight-year-old bachelor, has lived in the same apartment for five years. He has recently been laid off. For the past month, Joe has been trying to find another job. He has gone on interviews, gone to employment agencies, answered ads in the local newspaper. He has been careful about his bills. To avoid a bad credit rating, Joe has paid a small amount on each of his three credit cards and other bills. He has asked his landlady, Sara Western, for an extension on his rent. She agreed to give him an additional two weeks.

The Scenario:

The next morning Joe left for an interview for a job in a town 50 miles away. If he got the job it would be a 100-mile drive every day. "At least it would be a job," Joe mused as he returned to his apartment. As he climbed the steps he thought, "The drive wasn't that bad." He inserted his key into the door lock and it wouldn't work. He was stunned that he could not get into his apartment.

The lock had been changed. Joe went back downstairs, knocked on the land lady's apartment. She refused to come to open the door.

"Pay up or move out.! You don't get your stuff until you pay your rent."

"I don't understand. You said you'd give me an extra two weeks," Joe said.

"Go away," Sara grumbled.

Joe called a friend and made arrangements to stay overnight. The next morning he called the local authorities and was told they could do nothing about it. Joe then called an attorney who agreed to take the case pro bono. A suit was brought against Sara Western.

In court, Sara's attorney simply said that the tenant was past due in rent and management had denied access to the apartment until the past due rent was paid.

"Under state law, a landlord cannot use do-it-yourself eviction," Judge Hawthorne said. "Furthermore, he continued, "a landlord is specifically prohibited from preventing a tenant from gaining reasonable ace to his domicile by any means."[84]

INTERACTIVE THIRTY-ONE

Directions:

Complete each of the following listed areas and then in an essay apply Humanitarian Ethics to the case.

Primary Moral Issue:
Primary Moral Principle:
Alternatives:
Preferred Alternative:
Ethical Theory:
Justification:

Note: There are additional case studies for practice in Appendix Two.

***

GLOSSARY OF TERMS

Logical Priority . . . One of two ways in which human beings may prioritize their moral principles based on logic and empirical evidence.

Nonlocality . . . The principle that something can be affected in the absence of a local cause.

Particular Priority . . . The second way in which moral principles may be prioritized based on actual situations or context in which moral actions and decisions occur.

Principle of Goodness and Rightness . . . All persons should strive to be good and should attempt to carry out "right" actions.

Principle of Individual Freedom . . . Human beings are free to make choices in the ways and means by which they are moral within the framework of the first four principles of Humanitarian Ethics.

Principle of Justice and Fairness . . . The distribution of good and bad should be distributed on a fair and just basis.

Principle of Truth Telling and Honesty . . . Telling the truth and being honest is essential for any relationship whether personal, business or governmental.

Value of Life Principle . . . Human beings should revere life and accept death.

SUGGESTED READINGS

Alexander, Richard. **The Biology of Moral Systems**. Piscataway, N.J. Transaction Publishers. 1987

Feinberg, J. Doing and Deserving: Essays in Theory of Responsibility. Princeton. Princeton University Press, 1970

Flew, Antony. **Social Life and Moral Judgment**. Piscataway, N.J. Transaction Publishers, 2003

Decety, Jean and Thalia Wheatly. **The Moral Brain**. Cambridge. MIT Press. 2015

Goswami, Amit (with Richard E. Reed & Maggie Goswami**). The Self-Aware Universe**. New York. G. P. Putnam's Sons

Hinman, Lawrence M. "Interlude: Theories Against Theories-Recent Developments" in **Ethics: A Pluralistic Approach to Moral Theory**. San Diego. Harcourt Brace College Publishers, 1994

Rosenbaum, Thane. **The Myth of Moral Justice**. New York. Harper Collins. 2011

Thiroux, Jacques. **Ethics: Theory and Practice, Fifth Edition**. Englewood Cliffs. Prentice-Hall, 1995

Zohar, Danah (in collaboration with I. N. Marshall). **The Quantum Self**. New York. Quill (William Morrow), 1990

APPENDIX ONE

List of environmental issues[85]

Environmental issues are issues related to human impact on the living environment, habitats, land use, and natural resources.

The following alphabetical list shows some of the main known environmental issues by major topic title:

Acidification (includes algal bloom, coral reef loss, etc.)

Air quality (air pollution, ozone pollution, ties to human health with asthma, diesel emissions, etc.)

Biodiversity (conservation of biological diversity)

Climate change (encompasses "global warming", greenhouse effect, loss of glaciers, climate refugees, climate justice, equity, etc.)

Conservation (nature and animal conservation, etc.)

Consumerism (linking the state of consumers within the economy to environmental degradation and social malaise, planned obsolescence)

Deforestation (illegal logging, impact of fires, the rapid pace of destruction, etc.)

Desertification

Eco-tourism

Endangered species / threatened species (CITES, loss of species, the impact of chemical use on species, cultural use, species extinction, invasive species, etc.)

Energy (use, conservation, extraction of resources to create energy, efficient use, renewable energy, etc.)

Environmental degradation

Environmental health (poor environmental quality causing poor health in human beings, bioaccumulation, poisoning)

Environmental impact assessment (one major current form of assessing human impact on the environment)

Genetic engineering or modification (includes GMOs)

Global environmental issues (in recognition that environmental issues cross borders)

Grassroots solutions (local and regional environmental issues solved from the bottom-up)

Habitat loss (destruction, fragmentation, changed use)

Intergenerational equity (recognition that future generations deserve a healthy environment)

Invasive species (weeds, pests, feral animals, etc.)

Land degradation

Land use planning / Land use (includes urban sprawl)

Natural catastrophes (linked to climate change, desertification, deforestation, loss of natural resources such as wetlands, etc.)

Nuclear power, waste, and pollution

Over-exploitation of natural resources (plant and animal stocks, mineral resources (mining), etc.)

Overfishing (depletion of ocean fish stocks)

Ozone depletion (CFCs, Montreal Protocol)

Pollution (air, water, land, toxic, light, point source, and non-point source, use of coal/gas/etc., reclaimed land issues)

Population issues (overpopulation, access to reproductive control (reproductive health), etc.)

Reduce, reuse, recycle (and refuse) (ways to reduce impact, minimize footprint, etc.)

Soil conservation (includes soil erosion and salinization of land, especially fertile land; see also desertification and deforestation)

Sustainability (finding ways to live more sustainably on the planet, lessening human footprint, increasing human fulfillment with less impact) (see also sustainable development and poverty alleviation)

Toxic chemicals (persistent organic pollutants, prior informed consent, pesticides, endocrine disruptors, etc.)

Waste (landfills, recycling, incineration, various types of waste produced from human endeavors, etc.)

Water pollution (freshwater and ocean pollution, Great Pacific Garbage Patch, river and lake pollution, riparian issues)

Whaling (a specific issue due to its worldwide nature, treaties and persistent campaigns to prevent it; other cetaceans also impacted)

APPENDIX TWO

CREATING A CASE STUDY[86]

Reading about ethical theories and their originators provide a basis for you to become involved in the application of those theories. Remember, the focus throughout the book has been to give you practice in making moral and ethical decisions; not to convert you to a specific belief system of philosophical viewpoint. None of you can live all possible experiences in the world, even though you may feel that way sometimes. You can gain insights through means other than direct experience. One such way is through the use of case studies.

The case study, a unique device for gathering and presenting information, profiles a moral dilemma and provides you practice in making moral/ethical decisions based on that profile. Many times a case study will be based on actual historical events, others will be fictive. There will be times when you personally do not like a particular case and at such time you may find it difficult to make a judgment. However, you are expected to make a judgment anyway. It's practice. Remember, your judgments are based on the information made available to you in the case studies; it is not a personal commitment and you should not view it as such. For example, you may be asked to choose a preferred outcome in a moral dilemma, which approves abortion when in reality you are very much opposed to abortion. In these situations, the focal point is not to convert you to another set of beliefs, but to have you look at another perspective.

You have worked with case studies in the previous chapters. It is helpful to see the entire preparation outline for building a case study. Each of the main stations of the outline is explained. Following the outline is an example. A full case study used in the example is presented. Appendix Three contains additional case studies for your practice.

Setting Up A Case Study

Definition of Problem
This is a statement of what the problem is and contains the answers to these questions: What has happened and who is involved? How are those involved related or connected? How urgent is the time factor for those making the decision? Here consider the question of life/death, success/failure, or happiness/unhappiness. What is the basic conflict (problem) that must be dealt with?

Identification

This is a statement of who has to deal tithe the problem and should include the answers to these questions: Is more than one person involved? What is their connection and what role does each play? At this point, consider only the important aspects of the case. Your statement(s) should answer these questions: What feeling are operating within those involved? What are the apparent active moral issues? What is the moral issue and what I the moral principle involved?

Generate alternative choices

This is a crucial area because it involves proposed alternatives for the main character in the scenario. At least three options should be listed and each should be evaluated in terms of its moral value, not some off- the- wall whim.

State your preferred alternative

In a clear concise statement, write your choice of a solution to the moral issue presented in the scenario; give reasons for your choice. Comments such as "I felt it was right," are not acceptable.

Ethical theory

This statement identifies the actual ethical theory illustrated in the scenario. It is specific such as Utilitarianism or Divine Command, for example.

Justification of theory choice.

An explanation of why you made the choice you did. This will be about a paragraph in length in which you explain how the theory applies to the case.

Case Study Example

I. Definition of Problem
David, working for a local construction company as an auditor, catches some of the employees stealing expensive tools. Because the job is nearly complete, David has to decide to turn them or not turn them in.

II. Identification
David has to deal with problem of thievery. Even though he is not the men's supervisor, he is the accountable to the company's owner for accurate records, and audit.

III. Consideration of data
David's responsibility to his employer, to himself, and to the men involved is crucial. The crew resent him because they view him as a company spy. The moral issue involved is should one report the thievery when it is known? The moral principle is one should report thievery when it is known.

IV. Alternatives
David turns to his computer and pretends he sees nothing. David tells the men he is reporting them unless they return the stolen tools. David reports the men to his boss and lets him handle it.

V. Preferred Outcome
David reports the men to his boss and lets him handle it.

VI. Ethical Theory
Kant's Duty Ethics applies here.

VII. Justification of Theory Choice
Kant's Duty Ethics applies to this case because his "Categorical Imperative" simply stated asserts that an act is immoral if the rule that authorizes it cannot be made into a rule for all human beings. Stealing cannot be made moral because it cannot be applied to all people; thus stealing is immoral. Consequently, one is duty bound not to steal. If David had not reported the men who were stealing, he would have been a part of the theft. He had a duty, an obligation to be honest and report the situation to his boss.

Caution, Pitfalls Ahead:

There are some pitfalls in creating your own case studies. The first in writing a statement of *the primary moral issue*. This is actually a question and it must be phrased as a question. It raises the moral issue. Here are three examples.

Does one have the right to kill another human being?

Is lying ever acceptable?

Should one always be honest?

A second pitfall may show up in writing the *primary moral principle*. This is a statement that answers the question posed by the primary moral issue. Using the first example in the list, (Does one have the right to kill another human being?) the primary moral principle would be stated as follows: **It is wrong to kill another human being**. Notice that this is a very specific and strong statement. It is a moral judgment!

The third and last pitfall is found in the way alternatives are to be written. Because several things often stand in the way of the necessary effectiveness, writing alternatives is not always easy. There are three issues involved in writing alternatives.

Passive voice uses verb forms that bypass or de-emphasize the subject (the actor) and focuses on the object. This gives the impression that the object just sit there, passively, while something happens to it. For example; "The Ball was hit by Joan."

Active voice clearly names the subject and his or her actions. For example, "John hit the ball." Notice the very distinct difference between the two examples.

The first problem here is the failure to identify who is having an ethical dilemma. Who is faced with making the decision? The answer to this question identifies the person with the moral dilemma. Once this has been established you may begin to consider alternatives. The second problem in writing alternatives has to do with language. Alternatives are not be written in the past tense (John told his parents). The action (the verb and its complement) must reflect an ongoing process. The third issue in writing alternatives continues the involvement of language. Alternatives are to be sated only on the active voice, not in the passive voice. The shaded box above provides a short definition of these two terms. Be sure to state your alternatives in the active voice. After you have completed a couple of case outlines, it may not be necessary for you to do so for every case study you create. Where are to you find information for a case study and once you have completed the preparation outline, how are to you present your case study?

Basic information for your case studies may come from actual situations reported in the media, personal experience, work-related, or maybe completely fictionalized. If you use material from the media or based on personal experience, be sure to changes names, dates, times, and places. This is essential to insure the rights of others. Below is a presentation model for you to follow. Note the following instructions and that they are represented in the model.

At the top left of a sheet of paper or on a page in your word processor include the following information. (Do this only if you are working with a teacher who may require this as a homework assignment.)

Name, date of the study, the topic of the study, and source of information, and the case study number. (You assign the case a number.)

Fill in each of these areas: background data, the scenario, the statement of the primary moral issue, the statement of the primary moral principle, the actual outcome (if this was based on a real situation in which the outcome is known), your preferred outcome, the ethical theory involved, and your justification for the choices of theories.

The following case was used in the previous outline illustration.

AN EXAMPLE OF A CASE STUDY

Name: J.J. Jones
Date: 12/5/16
Topic: Stealing
Source: David
Case Number: 1

Background Data:

David Horseman, an auditor for Built Right Corporation, a local construction company, has the reputation of being overly scrutinizing when it came to the company's purchases and expenditures. Part of his job is to inventory all equipment. He checks billings to make sure the company has not been charged for services and goods not received.

One of the subcontractor's crews is hostile toward David. They are sure he reports them for taking too long a lunch break. They have lodged a complaint against him.

David and his wife Sharon are expecting their first child. The pregnancy has not been an easy one. His boss has promised him a much-needed bonus if he saved the company money through careful auditing.

The Scenario:

David was aware of the complaint lodged against him and it made him more cautious in checking purchases, timesheets, and other expenditures. He caught a $3,000 overcharge by the subcontractor whose crew had lodged the complaint against him. The charge was for the rental of a large piece of equipment that had not been used by his employer. David's boss and company owner, Bob Rhodes, was delighted with David's diligence. He was given a $300 bonus.

When confronted, the subcontractor quickly blamed the mischarge on his bookkeeper. This episode increased the hostility toward David. The subcontractor made no bones about his dislike for David.

As the job began to wind down, David began to notice an increase in the number of requisitions for replacement of tools. Suspicious, he set up a small surveillance camera in the trailer used to store small equipment. Three members of the subcontractor's crew were taking the equipment.

"Man, now what," David thought as he rewound the tape. "Should I confront them and give them a chance to return the equipment or just let Rhodes take care of it?"

The Primary Moral Issue:
Should one always report thievery?

The Primary Moral Principle:
One should always report thievery.

Alternatives:
David destroys the tape and says nothing

David confronts the men and tells them he is reporting them unless they return the equipment

David shows his boss the security tape and leaves it up to him as to what should be done.

The Actual Outcome:

David reported the incident and turned the tape over to his boss.

The Preferred Outcome:

In this situation, the preferred outcome is alternative number three. David reported the incident to his boss.

The Ethical Theory:

Kant's "Duty Ethics" is applicable to this case. His "Categorical Imperative" simply stated asserts that an act is immoral if the rule that authorizes it cannot be made into a rule for all human beings Stealing cannot be made moral because it cannot be applied to all people; thus, stealing is immoral. Consequently, one is duty-bound not to steal. If David had not reported the men who were stealing from the company, he would have been part of the thievery. He had a duty, an obligation to be honest and report the thievery.

APPENDIX THREE

PRACTICE CASE STUDIES

Case Study: Tiffany and Bob

Background Data:

Tiffany is twenty years old and is to marry Bob Glover within a week. She is involved in an automobile accident and is paralyzed from the neck down. Besides other serious injuries, she will never walk again, will lead a life of constant pain if she survives the massive surgery required to put her back together. The driver of the truck that rammed her vehicle was drunk and high on pot.

The Scenario:

Tiffany, driving home from a bridal shower, was enjoying her new convertible. As she sang along with her favorite group, she was unaware of the tractor-trailer behind her. Because she had been in a hurry to get home she had not fastened her seat belt and was thrown from her car. It rolled over on top of her causing massive injuries to her spine, internal organs, and head.

The truck careened off the road, plowing up a large scar in the embankment. The driver was not hurt.

The police arrested the driver for being under the influence. Tiffany was airlifted to a local hospital.

Bob Glover rushed to the hospital when he learned of Tiffany's accident. There, a doctor told him, Tiffany, if she survived additional surgery, would be paralyzed. Additionally, her larynx was crushed and she might never speak and if she did it might not be understandable. Her recovery was not promising.

As Bob and the doctor walked into Tiffany's room, they noticed a finger move.

"Just a twitch. Normal for situations like this," the doctor said replying to Bob's quizzical look.

Bob leaned over Tiffany and gently kissed her on the forehead. His eyelids shuddered. Her lips began to move.

"Let me die."

The doctor looked at Bob, shook his head. Fighting the tears, Bob left the hospital. He was devastated.

"What good is life without Tiffany?" Bob heard himself whisper.

"It isn't!" Bob said aloud.

Later that evening Bob returned to the hospital. He had a beautiful bouquet of roses with him, long-stemmed yellow roses. They were Tiffany's favorite. He kissed her and she opened her eyes. Tears formed and spilled down her cheeks. She struggled to open her lips.

"Help me die. Please!"

Bob leaned forward, gently kissed her, and pulled a gun from the bouquet of roses. He shot her once, in the head, killing her instantly. He put the gun into his mouth, squeezed the trigger, and slumped over the bed.

The Interactive:

Identify each of the following: The primary moral issue, the primary moral principle, four alternatives, your preferred outcome.

What is the philosophy involved in this case?

Case Study: Jackie vs Shirley

Background:

Jackie Widmore was completing her dissertation in microbiology. She worked in the same lab as another doctoral candidate. As the time grew closer to the completion date, Jackie wondered why Shirley was seldom in the lab. On several occasions Jackie found research materials addressed to Shirley unopened or crumpled up.

Jackie had the awful feeling that Shirley was not doing her research and was faking her results.

Both women shared the same dissertation advisor, Dr. Rudolf.

Shirley was a favorite of Dr. Rudolf and he had helped her on several research problems she had been having. Jackie would need the advisor's letter of recommendation for future positions to which she might apply. If she blew the whistle on Shirley that could jeopardize her degree and her entire future.

Jackie and Dr. Rudolf were using Shirley's research results in their own work. If Shirley's results were inaccurate it would cause serious professional issues for her as well as Dr. Rudolf. If she doesn't speak up now and informs Dr. Rudolf of her suspicions she would be challenged later as to why she hadn't spoken up.

Interactive:

Using the above information create a case study in which the dilemma is brought to a resolution. In your scenario, you may have Jackie and Shirley in a confrontational episode or you may have Jackie talking with Dr. Rudolf. Follow the standard procedure for creating a case study. Add these components:

Dialogue
Primary moral issue
Primary moral principle
Alternatives for Jackie
Ethical theory
Justification for your theory selection.

Case Study: Bonnie Jo vs Mrs. Lions

Background Data:

Bonnie Joe Hall is 38 years old and is a close friend of Alice Kempt, the mother of Jimmy, a mature 14-year-old

Last summer, Alice permitted Jimmy to stay with Bonnie Joe, thinking it would be good for her son to live in another state for a while. As the summer neared its end, Alice learned that Bonnie Joe had been giving Jimmy alcohol and drugs. To her horror, she learned that Bonnie Joe had been having sex with her son.

Angry, upset, and hurt by her friend's behavior and betrayal of trust, Alice bought a plane ticket and demanded that Jimmy is sent home. Jimmy refused to leave his "older woman." Rather than go back to his mother, Jimmy ran away but was later caught and returned to his mother.

In September, Bonnie Joe drove to Arizona, found Jimmy, and took off with him. For eight months the two moved from state to state, changing their names, hair color, and automobiles. Finally, Bonnie Joe was arrested in South Carolina. Jimmy was with her and a newborn child, Bonnie Joe claimed was Jimmy's.

Case Study: Robert vs State

Background Data:

Robert Yahn is 22 years old and has a serious congenital heart condition. His doctors say he should have a heart transplant. Robert has an IQ of around 73. The state has refused to give him necessary follow-up care because it does not consider him retarded. As a consequence, Robert is being denied a heart transplant.

Robert's lawyers have argued that he is retarded and that without aftercare, the day-to-day necessities after surgery such as taking medicine, eating properly, and keeping his medical appointments, he could not survive.

Case Study: Peter, Sandy, and Marcia

Background Data:

Peter and Sandy have tried for three years to conceive a child. They have not been successful. Doctors finally determined that Sandy could not have children. She is heartbroken.

Marcia, Sandy's older sister who is 45, tells Peter and Sandy that she is willing to be a surrogate. She is inseminated by in vitro. Marcia delivers healthy twin boys.

Who has legal custody?

Case Study: Garry Vs All Saints Christian School

Background Data:

Garry Troutman, a fourth-grade teacher at All Saints Christian School has been fired. The reason stated in his dismissal letter included the statement that he had let his teaching credentials lapse and that he had violated All Saint's expectations of teacher behavior and morality because his son was born two months early. The letter continued that the school did not approve of "shot-gun marriages."

Garry and his wife, Margie were shocked. Garry made a public statement that he was more than willing to go before the church and ask for forgiveness. He also noted he and Margie were married in the church that ran the school.

The school's chief administrator, at a public hearing, made the following statement: "We are a Christian school and we believe there should be consequences for a person's behavior. Admittedly, it is different than many other places in the world. It doesn't make any difference what one's personal life is out there, but in our world, it does."

After the hearing before the church and the school board and in consultation with an attorney, Garry went public, claiming he was discriminated against and that he was denied forgiveness.

ENDNOTES

1 Most states provide laws governing what constitutes justifiable homicide. An abused spouse, who kills her abuser in self-defense, depending on the situation, serves as an example.

[2] Hume goes on to say that, judgments of fact, as judgments concerning relations of ideas, are inactive; that is, they can never, by themselves, produce or prevent any action. On the other hand, judgments of value can do so. Reason, supplies the motive; it tells you to seek what you desire.

[3] Also included on Ross's list are gratitude, beneficence, self-improvement, and non-malfeasance.

[4] Roszak, Theodore. 1969. *The Making of a Counter Culture: Reflections on the Technocratic Society*. Garden City: Doubleday & Company, Inc.

[5] Sometimes the Principle of Unity is written as "the greatest good for the greatest number."

[6] For more a detailed discussion of this classification, see C.D. Broad's article, "Some of the Main Problems in Ethics" in ***Philosophy, Vol. 21***, 1946.

[7] A maxim or apothegm is a principle.

[8] Inegalitarianism is the view held by Nietzsche that not all rational beings are equally valuable. You may wish to read more about his "Master Morality.

[9] Ayn Rand. 1964. ***The Virtue of Selfishness: A New Concept of Egoism***. New York: Signet Books, The New American Library.

[10] Any Rand. 1963. ***For the New Intellectual.*** New York: Signet Books, The New American Library.

[11] Ibid. p. 25

[12] The Utility Principle is also called the Greatest Happiness Principle.

[13] Ellen Adams is a fictional character. Her story is based on an actual case in the State of Florida. The dialogue in the scenario is the creation of the author.

[14] For a more detailed discussion of this issue I suggest you read Austin Fagothey's Right Reason, revised by Milton A. Gonsalves (8th ed.), 1985.

[15] If an action were reversed, would you want it done to you? This is the idea of the "Golden Rule" as presented in Christianity.

[16] The morality of Plato's time would be considered immoral by many in today's world; particularly in the area of human sexuality.

[17] Other works by Nietzsche include Thus Spake Zarathustra (1883), Beyond Good and Evil (1886), The Gay Science, (1882-1887), The Genealogy of Morals (1887), and Twilight of the Idols (1888).

[18] Also called "superman". It was not a term created by Nietzsche. It appears in classical as well as German literature before Nietzsche. He, however, made it an essential part of his philosophy, which was a new application of the term.

[19] This statement appears in the opening of Nietzsche's *Thus Spake Zarathustra.*

[20] As quoted in **Elements of Moral Philosophy**. James Rachels. P. 17. Originally in Folkways by William Graham Sumner. Boston. Ginn & Company. 1906, p. 28.

[21] For a detailed discussion of legal rights, see Ronald Dworkin's ***Taking Rights Seriously***. Cambridge: Harvard University Press, 1977. Dr. Dworkin's work is considered significant in the area of jurisprudence. He is a critic of the legal positivists theory of rights.

[22] These constitute the Principle of Life. More will be said about this in a later chapter.

[23] *The Journal of Philosophy, Vol.LXI, no 20*(Oct. 29, 1964) reprinted in Norman E. Bowie's Making Ethical Decisions. New York: McGraw-Hill Company, 1985, pp. 210-16.

[24] Based on an actual case. As with other case studies, the names have been changed to protect the rights of those involved. Additionally, some circumstances have been fictionalized.

[25] Diversity and its moral implication will be discussed under a separate heading.

[26] Act IV, Scene One, ***The Merchant of Venice***. William Shakespeare. Interlinear Edition prepared by George Coffin Taylor and Reed Smith. Boston. Ginn and Company, 1962, lines 180-192, pp. 104-105.

[27] From "The Basis and Content of Human Rights" by Alan Gewirth reprinted in ***Making Ethical Decisions*** by Norman E. Bowie. New York: McGraw Hill Book Company, 1985, p0. 219

[28] Alasdair MacIntyre, *After Virtue, Seconds Edition*. Notre Dame: Notre Dame University Press, 1984, p. 244.

[29] Harcourt Brace College Publishers. New York: 1994, see chapter eleven.

[30] Involved the question of what could be taught in a public school, specifically the Theory of Evolution by Darwin.

[31] Study by Carmela Lomonaco, Tia Kim, and Lori Ottaviani. Southern California Academic Center of Excellence on Youth Violence Prevention, University of California, Riverside.

[32] Named for United States Attorney General, Edwin Meese. The Commission made a study of experiments that had been conducted by various groups in the social sciences.

[33] Quoted in "The Sunny Side of Smut" by Melinda Wenner Moyer *in Scientific American Mind Behavior &Society*, July 1, 2011.

[34] Natalie Angier, "Sexual harassment: Why even bees do it: The New York Times, printed in The Lakeland Ledger, Oct. 15, 1995, Section G. P. 5 under "Science and Technology."

[35] Issued by the Sacred Congregation for the Doctrine of Faith, Dec. 29, 1975

[36] From *Right Conduct: Theories and Applications*. Michael D. Bayles and Kenneth Henley, ed. New York: Random House, 1983, p. 211. Modified to meet the "case study" approach in this book.

[37] Abramson, Paul and Steven Pinkerton. With Pleasure: Thoughts on the Nature of Human Sexuality. New York. Oxford University Press, 1995.

[38] From *Bad Subjects # 17* November 1994, c. by Annalee Newitz, 1993.

[39] John Stoltenberg, Refusing to be a Man: Essays on Sex and Justice. New York. Meridian, 1989.

[40] op.cit.

[41] Based on Stoltenberg's book, Refusing to be a Man: Essays on Sex and Justice.

[42] Based on a famous 1985 case. Names of persons, places, and circumstances have been changed to protect those involved. Dialogue has been created by the author.

[43] Based on an actual case in 1989. Names of persons, places, and some circumstances have been changed to protect the rights of those involved.

[44] The full quotation by Dr. Carlos Gomez reads as follows: "Assisted suicide represents "the yuppicification of death: I want it my way, when I want it and without any complications." Quoted in Amy Goldstein's article, "Conscious Will or Yuppicification of Death?" *Washington Post* reprinted in *The Seattle Times*, April 4th, 199t6 section A21.

[45] ***Summa Theologia***, 1-11,Q.94,a2 & 11-11,Q.58, a.1.

[46] John Lock, ***Second Treatise of Government***, Chap. 4, sec. 23, & chp. 15, sec. 172.

[47] Immanuel Kant, *Metaphysical Elements of Justice* (John Ladd, trans.). Indianapolis. Bobs-Merrill, 1965, pp. 35 & 45.

[48] For a more detailed discussion of social justice read Archie J. Aaham's *Why Be Moral?* Albuquerque. World Books, 1992, chp. 20.

[49] Sagan, Carl. "Pulling the Plug on Mother Earth." In State Government News, the Council of State Governments, 1991.

[50] "Ethics and the Environment" in *Ethics and Problems of the 21st Century.* Goodpaster and Sayer, eds. 1979, 3-119 as quoted in *Contemporary Moral Problems*. James E. White. St. Paul: West Publishing, 1985, 303-315.

[51] In *Environment*, Oct. 1995, Vol. 37, N.8, 5-29

[52] A modification of a chart in O'Riordan "Frameworks of Choice: Core Beliefs and the Environment" in *Environment. Oct. 1995, Vol. 37 No. 8, 7*

[53] www.peta.org/issues/animals-used-for-experimentation/animals-used-experimentation-factsheets/animal-experiments-overview/

[54] Based on Jim Manson's "Following the Waters" in *E Magazine.* Oct. 1995, Vol. VI, N. 5, 33.

[55] Wikipedia.org. "Flint Water Crisis," August 18, 2016

[56] ABC News. WNEM-TV. "Flint Water Crisis", January 1, 2016.

[57] From a report issued November 13, 1995 at the International Conference on Biodiversity, Jakarta, Indonesia.

[58] From Internet Activities Board, "Communications of the ACM, Vol. 32, NO. 6, June, 1989, Vint Cerf. (Last updated 94/12/06. Reprinted [on the NET] with permission of the ACM under the blanket agreement to the Virginia Tech Educational Infrastructure Grant, 1993. Downloaded from the NET, March 19, 1996.

[59] Ibid

[60] The Court issued a temporary restraining order against the enforcement of the law. However, in writing his decision, the judge wrote, "The defendant, her agents, and her servants are hereby ENJOINED from enforcing against plaintiffs the provisions of 47 U.S.C. Section 223 (A) (1) (B) (ii), insofar as they extend to "indecent," but not "obscene." The plaintiff's motion is in all other respects DENIED.

[61] Based on an actual case reported by Woody Baird of the Associated Press, in the "Seattle Times," Feb. 1976. The author has changed the names of the couple as well as the city of the inspector to protect their rights

[62] Daniel Loeffler, 10/05/94. Printed on the Internet in Word Codes.

[63] **Journal of Health, Law and Public Policy, Spring, 1995**. Institute of Medicine. Health Data in

the Information Age: Use, Disclosure, and Privacy," Washington, DC: National Academy Press, 1995.

[64] Mr. Barlow is a retired cattle rancher, author, co-founder and executive chair of the Electronic Frontier Foundation, and a lyricist for the Grateful Dead.

[65] John Perry Barlow, "The Economy of Ideas", 1993, 4. Ventures USA Ltd. WIRED online, p. 1 of the download.

[66] Op.cit

[67] Originally published in The Times Higher Education Supplement, June 9, 1995, p. 3.

[68] Op.cit.

[69] A modified version based on an article in **Business Ethics Magazine, January/February, 1996**, "What Would You Do? Burned by the System: When the Boss's Success Comes at the Expense of Others." Copyright, 1996, Business Ethics Magazine.

[70] **Ethics: A Pluralistic Approach to Moral Theory**. San Diego: Harcourt Brace College Publishers, 1994.

[71] Thiroux, James P. **Ethics: Theory and Practice, 11th Ed.** New York: Pearson, 2015.

[72] Based on an actual case. Names and locations have been changed to protect the rights of those involved. Dialogue was created by the author. This was a pioneering case because the area of privacy in terms of voice mail was vague. Privacy is established on the telephone and written mail. A court order is required to listen to your

conversations and/or to read your mail. The same issues were faced with the advent of email.

[73] Creativity Research Journal, Vol. 6 (1&2) 185-196, (1993).

[74] Campbell, Joseph. *Myths to Live By*. New York: Bantam Books, Inc. 1972, p. 9.

[75] Creativity Research Journal. (see end note 76) p.186.

[76] Amit Goswami is the author of The Self-Aware Universe, The Concepts of Physics, Quantum Mechanics, The Cosmic Dancers, Physics of the Soul, and Quantum Creativity.

[77] Zohar, Danah (with I .N .Marshall). *The Quantum Self: Human Nature and Consciousness Defined by the New Physics.* New York: Quill (William Morrow), 1990, p. 35.

[78] Ibid. p. 187

[79] Transcendence generally means lying beyond the ordinary range of perception. In Kant's Theory of Knowledge it is used to mean beyond the limits of experience and hence unknowable. It also means being above and independent of the material universe. It is this last definition is the most likely application here.

[80] Ibid. p. 191
[81] Ibid. p. 191-192
[82] Ibid. p. 193
[83] Ibid. p. 195

[84] This modified case happened in Florida. Under Florida statute, a landlord who has just cause to evict a tenant for non-payment of rent must give the

tenant a three-day notice to pay the amount due or vacate. If the tenant fails to perform as required under the notice, the property owner must then file a complaint for eviction for the non-payment of rent in the county court where the property is located. The names of the characters and the dialogue are creations of the author.

[85] From http://www.appropedia.org

[86] The image of the man in a hat pointing is from www.publicdomainvectors.org.

www.ingramcontent.com/pod-product-compliance
Lightning Source LLC
Chambersburg PA
CBHW010855090426
42737CB00019B/3368